Introduction

PHEW! That was an action-packed millennium by any standards.

A North Yorkshire resident, watching dawn break on New Year's Day 1000, could never have guessed what the future held. Unknown to him, the Viking empire was on its last legs. Within 70 years, the country would be under Norman rule.

And that was only the start. Fast forwarding through the years, it might seem that all they contained was bloodshed. From the Battle of Stamford Bridge in the millennium's first century to the Second World War in its last, and not forgetting the bloodiest single battle of them all, Towton, there has hardly been a break in the fighting.

But we must not forget the incredible advances that also took place. Over a period of 250 years, York Minster was built, a testament to man's skill and determination as well as a temple to his maker.

The Merchant Adventurers developed trade as never before; the sport of kings and commoners, horse racing, began on Knavesmire; the novel was invented almost single-handedly by a Yorkshire cleric called Sterne; water and power supplies were piped into York city centre; and the city saw its first newspaper.

And that is before we consider the 20th century, the most remarkable of them all. From flying machines to floods, Minster celebrations and conflagrations, North Yorkshire has had a remarkable last hundred years.

Only some of these events could be brought to you by the Evening Press. That newspaper arrived towards the end of this millennium.

This book fills that gap. The Millennium Press brings you the news of 50 historic events from 1066 on, as if our reporters had been present at every one of them. It makes for a dramatic read, as we hope you will agree.

Chris Titley and Martin Lacy

Millennium Press was written by Chris Titley and Martin Lacy and edited and designed by Martin Lacy. Cover design by Lisa Cook.

About the authors

CHRIS Titley has been a journalist for eight years. He first visited York on family trips from his Nottinghamshire home in the 1970s and can still recall the excitement of walking down Kirkgate in the Castle Museum.

He joined the Evening Press in York in 1993, later establishing the newspaper's popular local history feature Yesterday Once More. A collection of these features was later published in a book of the same name. He lives in York with his partner Jo and their young son Jack.

MARTIN Lacy is a native of York and has been a journalist for 31 years. He joined the Gazette & Herald in 1974 before transferring to the Evening Press sport desk in 1977, where he spent 11 years as the paper's rugby league writer.

He is currently Special Publications Editor at the Evening Press, a role that has involved him in the editing and production of several nostalgia publications including the York Then and Now and Yesterday Once More books.

A keen local historian, he is married with two grown-up children and a six-year-old grand-daughter who is already showing a healthy interest in the city's history.

Index to contents

Sources

The authors would like to thank the Evening Press library staff and the staff at both York Reference Library and the York City Archives for their help with this book.

A number of general reference works were consulted by the authors. Principally, these were:

A History of the City of York by Charles Brunton Knight, pub 1944
A History of the County of York edited by PM Tillott, 1961
The Noble City of York edited by Alberic Stacpoole, 1972

The Evening Press archives were another major source.

On individual subjects:
York Waterworks, 1677-1903: a short historical & descriptive account
Knavesmire: York's great racecourse & its stories by John Stevens, Pelham Books
A Long History of Horse Racing by AL Laishley in Yorkshire Illustrated, August 1952
Laurence Sterne – Coxwold's Novelist Parson by Margaret Ottley, The Yorkshire Ridings, December 1967
Bootham Park Hospital Bi-Centenary Programme
From York Lunatic Asylum to Bootham Park Hospital by Anne Digby, University of York Borthwick Paper no. 69
The History of the Ouse Bridge, York, by D Morrell in The Builder, May 1912
Brontëland link with Ouse Bridge Builder by Joe Stobbs in the Yorkshire Ridings Magazine, July 1971
A Century of Light: York Gas Company 1824-1924
York Times article, Spring 1963
The Horse Tramways of York by Hugh Murray
Yorkshire's Early Flying Days by Richard Nelson Redden
The York Blitz 1942 by Charles Whiting
The York Festival 1951 by PA Harrison in The York Historian

The Battle of Stamford Bridge
September 25, 1066

THE history of our nation has turned on a few crucial events, but perhaps the Battle of Stamford Bridge was the most crucial of all. A disgruntled member of the Saxon Royal family and a freebooting Viking combined to alter the face of English history.

Everyone knows about the Battle of Hastings in 1066, when the Saxon Kingdom of England was conquered by the Norman French, yet another battle fought almost 300 miles north of Hastings barely three weeks earlier played a vital part in the course of events.

England in 1066 was a hotbed of seething political infighting. The old King, Edward The Confessor, thought by many to be a saint, but generally despised by his contemporaries, had failed to provide an heir. Not only that but his political ditherings during his reign had left more than one powerful magnate eyeing the throne. A scattering of Vikings, Normans and Saxons all had claims but a Saxon, Harold Godwinson, was the man in possession.

Crowned in January, 1066, he had already put down a rebellion on the Welsh borders and faced trouble from Northumbria - a remnant of the old Viking Kingdom of York. York was the capital of Northumbria and a hotbed of Viking unrest. To deal with the problems, Harold sent his brother Tostig. Tostig's heavy handed efforts proved too efficient and the unhappy Northumbrians threw him out. When Harold refused to back his hothead brother, Tostig fled to Scandinavia to enlist the aid of former Byzantium mercenary, Harald Hardrada.

Hardrada had acquired the throne of Sweden and Norway and had Denmark on its knees. Now he fancied adding the English throne and in September, 1066, sailed up the River Ouse with Tostig and a massive fleet. They anchored at Riccall and marched on York, where the English forces were hammered at the Battle of Fulford.

It seems likely that there was some connivance between the invaders and the Viking inhabitants of York, for the city was not sacked and Hardrada felt safe enough to leave 5,000 of his troops and his armour at Riccall while he marched to Stamford Bridge to receive hostages. But the dustcloud he saw approaching from York was not the hostages but King Harold and his army - his professional bodyguard of Housecarls and the Fyrd, the Saxon conscript army gathered up by Harold as he marched north from London.

The Vikings were formidable warriors, but the Housecarls, armed with their deadly axes, were some of the most feared soldiers of their day and after a long struggle, in which Hardrada and Tostig were both slain, and the English had withstood a late counterattack by Viking reinforcements from Riccall, Harold was triumphant.

His triumph was short-lived. Soon after the battle he heard the news he had expected all summer - Duke William of Normandy had landed on the South Coast. Harold gathered up his battle-weary army and marched south - and the rest is history. A weakened Saxon army put up a brave struggle but in a close run affair came out second best - and Harold was killed. But how would English history have been changed if Hardrada and Tostig hadn't invaded and the Normans had had to face a brave Saxon warrior king and a fresh, professional army?

Millennium Press

September 25, 1066   **A thousand years of York's history**

Victory at Stamford Bridge

King Harold defeats Viking invaders

HAROLD Godwinson, King of England for less than a year, pulled off the greatest victory of his short reign today when he smashed a huge Viking army led by the giant Harald Hardrada, King of Sweden and Norway, and Harold's treacherous brother Tostig.

In a day-long battle in the lush water meadows alongside the River Derwent at the tiny village of Stamford Bridge, near York, Harold's brave and fearless Housecarls, backed by the loyal Saxon Fyrd, destroyed a Viking army that had already

English and Viking forces clash at Stamford Bridge today as King Harold took on the invading forces of the Swedish King, Harald Hardrada and the English King's renegade brother, Tostig. Victory went to the English, with both Hardrada and Tostig slain

beaten the Northern Earls Morkere and Edwin at Fulford and looked set to ravage the North of England.

Some 14,000 invaders, including Hardrada and Tostig were slain and the remnants of the invading army sailed back to

Scandinavia with their tails between their legs.

Late News

Norman hard man, Duke William the Bastard, reported to have landed in Sussex. King Harold immediately left York to face new threat.

Rebellion and a city in flames
1069

FOR a brief time in 1069, York once again was an independent kingdom. But it was to be the last real fling of rebellion and by the time Christmas came, the city and great tracts of land all around lay waste, savaged by vengeful Normans, and the Minster had been burned to the ground.

William's victory at Hastings in 1066 had seen the end of the House of Godwinson but not the Saxon resistance. In the south, William was able to control the conquered Saxons with some ease but in the North it was a different kettle of fish and he faced major problems. Soon after Hastings he had built a wooden castle on the site of the current Clifford's Tower and in 1069, as the political situation deteriorated and rebels besieged the garrison in York, he had marched north to scatter them and construct a second wooden castle on Baile Hill across the river.

A strong force was needed, for Robert of Comines and 900 Normans had been slaughtered after attempting to occupy Durham. Strong forces of opposition were about. Gospatrick, the deposed Saxon Earl of Northumberland, had joined forces with Edgar Atheling, grandson of King Edmund Ironside, and rightful heir to the throne of England. When they united with King Sweyn of Denmark, a nephew of King Canute and another with a claim to the throne of England, things looked black for King William.

The Danes met up with their English allies at the mouth of the Humber and marched on York. Before they arrived disaster struck the city. The Norman defenders decided to fire a few Saxon houses to give them clear fighting ground, the fire got out of control and the Saxon Minster was burned to the ground. The flames also consumed the great Minster library and the city records.

The Normans paid the price when the allies arrived. Commander William Malet decided to forsake his twin strongholds and marched the garrison out to meet them. They were slaughtered almost to a man, only Malet and a few other high-ranking Normans being spared for ransom.

For a brief spell, Sweyn had restored the old Viking Kingdom of York but it soon became apparent that his English allies would back the claims of Edgar Atheling rather than his own, so the disgruntled Danish king collected up his booty and sailed home.

Meanwhile, a furious William gathered his Army and marched north. Gospatrick and Atheling fled, leaving the city at the mercy of the Normans. The inhabitants got none. William embarked on a campaign of ethnic cleansing. Homes were burnt, crops ruined, livestock slaughtered. And Englishmen, whether of Saxon or Viking descent, were butchered simply because of their race – without trial and without mercy.

The North and York were left a wasteland and the great earldom of Northumberland split up among William's followers. Two men benefited in particular. His nephew, Alan of Brittany, gotg a vast tract of land in North Yorkshire, where he built Richmond Castle, and Ilbert de Lacy was granted what was virtually the old West Riding and built Pontefract Castle. These powerful magnates and their imposing castles eventually extinguished the flame of English rebellion in the North.

Millennium Press

A city in flames

Minster fired as Norman troops panic

YORK'S historic cathedral church, the Minster, lay today in smouldering ruins as an attempt by Norman troops to improve the city's defences went horribly wrong.

The recent slaughter of 900 Normans under Robert of Comines at Durham and the gathering of rebel forces at the mouth of the Humber, united Edgar Atheling, grandson of Edmund Ironside and the Saxon heir to the throne of England, Gospatrick, the deposed earl of Northumberland, with Sweyn, King of Denmark, and, as a nephew of King Canute, another with good claims to the throne of England.

William Malet, comman-

York's historic Minster goes up in flames after over-enthusiastic Norman troops' attempts to improve the city defences got out of hand

der of the Norman forces in York, faced with this large threat, ordered several commoners' houses to be fired to clear some fighting ground but the

plan went wrong when the fire burned out of control, finally setting the historic Saxon Minster alight and burning the church to the ground.

The Domesday Book and a city in ruins
1087

THE year of 1087 possibly marked the lowest point in the City of York's fortunes. The citizens lived in fear and poverty and much of the city was a wasteland, ravaged by the great fire and siege of 1069 and the 'Harrying of the North' carried out after the siege.

The great census of England, known as the Domesday Book, was published in 1087 and it reveals a dreadful picture. York in 1087 occupied an area within the current bar walls, with a few straggling houses alongside the main routes and some scattered villages such as Haxby and Strensall.

The Domesday Book provides much valuable information about William's England, although its original purpose was simply a rendition of all taxable property to enable the Norman taxgatherers to wring every available penny out of the downtrodden population.

York had been a thriving trading port and city of craftsmen in Viking times. It possessed a great church (the Minster), a court and palace for the Earls of Northumberland, and many flourishing export and import businesses. Ships sailed from its staiths all over northern Europe and foreign traders brought exotic goods to the city.

A century before the Norman invasion, it was estimated that the Danish and Saxon inhabitants numbered 30,000. By 1087, that prosperity had long disappeared, its population was well under 10,000, its great Minster a smoking ruin and many of the city's houses lay unoccupied or derelict.

The Domesday survey revealed that the city, divided into six shires or wards, one of which was owned by the Archbishop of York, contained just over 1,400 houses. Of these, however, only 391 were deemed fully taxable. Another 400 were so badly damaged as to only pay one penny in tax and yet another 145 were inhabited by Normans and as such tax-free. Some 540 were so derelict as to pay no tax at all.

York was a city in ruins, yet at this time the city possessed one of the finest church buildings in the country – not the Minster, destroyed by the disastrous fire of 1069, but St Mary's Abbey.

In 1080, the Norman, Alan of Brittany, perhaps feeling guilty about his leading part in the Harrowing of the North (but more likely simply wanting to promote Norman ways and institutions) had given four acres of land adjoining St Olave's Church for the foundation of a monastery, with Stephen named as the first abbot.

By all accounts the first abbey was a small affair, with perhaps as few as six monks, but greater glory was just round the corner. In 1087, the Archbishop of York, perhaps envious of a new religious building going up in York when his Saxon Minster was in ruins and many of his priests dead or fled, claimed the land was his. One of the first acts of William Rufus when he became king in 1087 was to visit York and in 1088 he not only settled the dispute in the abbey's favour but also granted the villages of Clifton and Overton to the abbey and laid the foundation stone for a new and grander abbey church (little of either of the Norman abbeys remain – the splendid ruins in the Museum Gardens are of the 13th century abbey).

While the new abbey had little benefit in the short term for the citizens of York, groaning under their Domesday Book tax burden, the foundation of such an impressive religious establishment marked the resurgence of York as the premier city of the North of England.

Millennium Press

1087   **A thousand years of York's history**

Tax shock for York citizens

Domesday Book reveals shocking state of city

KING William's great survey of this land of England, known as the Domesday Book, has revealed the shocking state of affairs in the second city of the nation.

The massive survey, published in two volumes - the Little Domesday, covering Essex, Norfolk and Suffolk, and the Great Domesday, covering the rest of the country south of the River Tees - shows just how much the events of recent years have hit the city.

The Anglo-Danish uprising of 1069 and the King's violent punishment of the whole of the North for their part in the uprising, has left the city devastated.

The Domesday Book reveals that of 1,400 houses in the city, 540 are so derelict as to pay no tax at all and another 400 will pay only one penny. The rest will foot the full tax bill, although some householders have already expressed anger that the 145 houses occupied by Normans would be tax exempt.

York's housing stock has been badly hit by war and rebellion, the Domesday Book reveals

York's Millennium Markets

Though there have been markets in York since the turn of the last Millennium, it was not until the 14th century that they were given the royal seal of approval. In 1316 Edward II granted the royal charter for markets and fairs in the City, which stated...

'whereas the said citizens and their ancestors have had in the absence of the King the assize of bread and ale, the assay of bread and ale, the assay of weights and measures and all other things belonging to the office of the market in the said City and suburbs, in the future they shall have the said assize assay and other things belonging to the office of the market in the King's presence and shall punish trespassers of the said assize..."

Over the centuries, a herb market, fish markets, general produce markets, cattle market, corn market and cloth market were spread around St Sampson's Square, Pavement, High Ousegate and Coppergate.

The last major move for the market was in April 1964 whereby, after 127 years in Parliament Street, the market transferred to it's now main site of Newgate, from where it's 120 stalls will see in the new millennium.

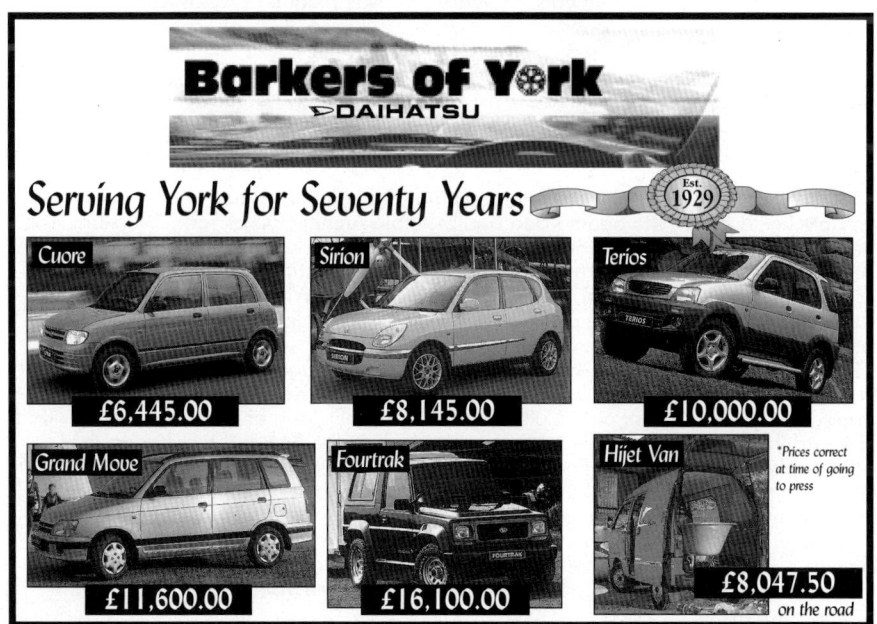

The Battle of Northallerton
August 22, 1138

*T*HE relationship between the citizens of York and the Scots has rarely been cordial down the centuries – so much so that for a long time Scotsmen were barred from holding any civic post in the city and there was even a by-law, supposedly never repealed, that allows native-born citizens of York to shoot (with a bow and arrow) any Scotsman he finds wandering abroad within the city walls in the hours of darkness!

The enmity between the two is not difficult to trace: since Roman times York was a frontier town, the last great city of England before you reached the 'badlands' on either side of the English-Scottish border.

Hundreds of battles and skirmishes were fought in Cumbria, Northumberland and Durham – and the Scottish Border regions – over the centuries as the two kingdoms fought over a variety of issues from land claims to sovereignty. York's role in these encounters was usually as a garrison town or point of muster, or even a base for kings such as Edward I, who made York his capital while he took on the Scots. But in 1138, York found itself very much in the war zone.

The Scottish attack came three years into the reign of the troubled King Stephen. Stephen, although grandson of William the Conqueror, had a feeble claim to the throne: the rightful heir was the headstrong and unpopular Matilda, daughter of the late king, Henry I. But the barons were in no mood to accept a woman and Stephen gained the throne with little opposition. Trouble immediately broke out with Matilda's supporters and much of Stephen's 19-year reign was plagued by civil war.

One of Matilda's early supporters was her uncle, David, King of Scotland – although it's hard to say whether he was really a champion of her cause or merely hoping to take advantage of the turmoil in England to seize lands and booty.

He had already invaded England in 1136, when Stephen had bought off his foes with various promises, including the Earldom of Northumberland for David's son. When the earldom wasn't forthcoming, David raised another army and marched south for York.

Stephen was in desperate straits in the South and could send few troops – but he had an able lieutenant in the ageing and bodily-feeble Archbishop of York, Thurstan. Despite the fact that the old man could barely stand and had to be carried in a litter, he succeeded in raising a formidable army, recruiting local levies and prompting the great landowners to take part, including Walter l'Espec, William de Percy, Richard de Stuteville, Roger de Mowbray and Robert de Brus, whose family was later to provide Scotland's most famous king.

The English marched north to meet the Scots and on August 22, 1138 the two armies met at Cowton Moor just north of Northallerton, the English rallying round a wagon flying the banners of St Cuthbert of Durham, St John of Beverley and St Wilfrid of Ripon (hence the alternative name for the clash of the Battle of the Standards).

The Scots charged into the English line first but were easily repulsed and when the English mounted a counter charge, the Scots fled. The battle was all over by 9am and only one man-at-arms on each side was killed.

The Scottish knights, showing less than gallantry, spurred their horses northwards, leaving their foot soldiers to fend for themselves and face the wrath of the English. For the rest of that summer day, the fields and streams of the Vale of York ran red with Scottish blood.

Millennium Press

August 22, 1138 · **A thousand years of York's history**

Scots routed!

Archbishop's army sees off Scottish invasion

A great victory has been won over the invading Scottish forces of King David just outside Northallerton.

The Northern earls, under the leadership of Archbishop Thurstan, and following the three banners of St Cuthbert of Durham, St John of Beverley and St Wilfrid of Ripon, smashed the Scots in a brief skirmish at Cowton Moor this morning.

King David's cowardly attack was launched when he knew that our noble King Stephen had his hands full dealing with rebel subjects in the South.

He claimed that Stephen had failed to honour promises made two years ago when the Scots launched another inva-

One of the English knights whose charge today routed the Scots at the Battle of Northallerton

sion of Northern England.

Presumably the treacherous Scottish king hoped for easy pickings - but he reckoned without the grit and courage of the ageing Archbishop.

Thurstan may be feeble in body (he had to be carried to the battle in a litter) but he is strong in spirit and his leadership encouraged the English forces to withstand the original Scottish charge

and then launch a battle-winning charge of their own - which routed the Scots.

Casualties are believed to be light - just one knight on each side - and most of the Scottish knights are believed to be galloping back to their homes. The common foot soldiers are likely to suffer retribution at the hands of the victorious English.

The massacre of York's Jewish population
March 16, 1190

THE darkest moment in York's long history came on the night of March 16, 1190, when the city's Jewish population was wiped out in Clifford's Tower, surrounded by a mob of York citizens baying for blood.

Although most of the 1,500 or more Jewish residents died by their own hand – only a few survivors being massacred by the mob – the responsibility for this moment of shame lies firmly at the door of the citizens and clergy of York.

Not all the blame should go their way, however, for the man ultimately responsible for this terrible persecution was King Richard I. The Lionheart, idolised by Victorian writers and Hollywood film-makers, was possibly the worst king to sit on England's throne. Vain, brutal, bigoted and cruel, he spent less than ten months of his ten-year reign in England, which he saw mainly as a treasure chest useful to finance his vainglorious military adventures in Europe and the Holy Land.

The Jews, who had arrived in England after the Norman Conquest, had a tough time at the hands of bigoted Englishmen, but had prospered under the reign of Richard's father, the wily Henry II, who welcomed the Jews' business acumen and utilised their wealth to obtain favourable loans. In return he encouraged their enterprise and as a result thriving Jewish communities grew up in cities around the country, including York.

Richard was nothing like his father. One of his first acts was to ban all Jews from his coronation. Several prominent Jewish citizens, wishing to pay their respects to the new king, ventured into the coronation banquet – and were driven out with great violence. Two of the Jews were from York – Benedict and Josias (or Jocenus) and Benedict later died from the beating he received.

When Josias returned to York he found that a mob, led by local creditors such as Richard Malebysse, Philip of Fauconberg, William Percy and Marmaduke Darrell and backed by soldiers waiting to go on a Crusade, had ransacked Benedict's house and murdered his wife and children.

Soon they were marching on Josias's house in Coney Street and he fled to the safety of the castle keep – then built of wood – along with his family and fellow Jews of York. Entreaties for mercy were ignored, as was the offer of a large cash sum for safe passage, and with the mob threatening to break in, the Jews decided on self-destruction rather than face the wrath of the citizens.

Men killed their wives and children before committing suicide. A few who lacked the resolution to kill themselves begged for mercy but were slaughtered to a man. Finally the castle keep was fired and the mob marched off to the Minster to seize the Jewish money-lending records and burn them.

When the smoke cleared, some 500 Jewish men, their wives and children – at least 1,500 souls – lay dead, victims of bigotry and greed.

Richard ordered an inquiry and some soldiers were dismissed and some lands seized but the ringleaders were able to reclaim their estates by paying a small fine. The blackest deed in York's history went virtually unpunished.

Millennium Press

Tragedy at York Castle

Suicide pact by city's Jews - death toll of 1,500

D ETAILS are now emerging of a bizarre suicide pact which has claimed the lives of virtually the entire Jewish community in York - around 1,500 men, women and children.

After weeks of unrest and rioting, the Jews went to the castle keep to seek sanctuary. When it became clear there would be no escape from the mob, which was apparently led by local men who were heavily in debt to Jewish moneylenders, the immigrant community decided on drastic measures. During the night, wives and children were killed

York Castle: the site of the massacre of the city's Jewish population

by their fathers and husbands, who then committed suicide.

The few Jews who survived threw themselves on the mercy of the mob but were murdered before the wooden keep was set on fire. It now lies in smouldering ruins.

An official enquiry has been started but there are already claims of a whitewash and it is feared that the killers will never be brought to justice.

The Signing of Magna Carta
June 15, 1215

*T*HE Magna Carta ("Great Charter") is one of the most important documents in English history, securing, as it does, rights we now take for granted, providing a basis for many of our laws and leading to the system of Parliamentary democracy we now enjoy.

Yet the part York and the magnates of the surrounding area played in the forcing of the document upon King John has long been forgotten.

When John ascended the throne in 1199 hopes were high for better times after the draining of the kingdom's wealth by the glory-seeking Richard, even if John was not the legitimate heir (that was his nephew, Arthur of Brittany, who was to die in mysterious circumstances while a prisoner of John). The desire for peace and prosperity persuaded the barons to overlook John's faults. They were soon to regret that. John was no madman, unlike his elder brother Richard, and inherited much of his father's cunning but the youngest of Henry II's four sons was devious, ill-tempered, untrustworthy and a noted lecher (he divorced his first wife to marry a 12-year-old girl, was accused of rape, and starved to death Matilda de Brose and her young son after the former allegedly resisted his amorous advances).

The famous Plantagenet temper got him into lots of trouble. He fell out with the clergy (then the country's civil service), the Pope, who placed an Interdict on England (no religious services could be conducted) and the monasteries.

But his greatest crime was to lose most of England's possessions in France in a series of disastrous military encounters over the first decade of his reign. That had three effects of the English nobility. Firstly, they were Anglo-Normans and many still had estates in France and the loss of Normandy in 1204 robbed them of these lucrative lands. Secondly, success in medieval warfare meant chances to collect hefty ransoms on captured opponents and thirdly, to pay for the wars, John increased scrutage, the cash tax levied in lieu of providing the king with troops. The burden fell particularly heavily on the North, with perhaps a quarter of the tax levied on an area containing just one sixth of the country's population.

This, plus John's habit of ignoring the laws of the land in his judgements, led to general unrest. But the move to curb John's actions was centred on the North and especially around York, which, either through desire or prudence, quickly sided with the rebels. Leading opponents included Ros at Helmsley, Stuteville at Kirkbymoorside and Cottingham, Percy at Whitby and Topcliffe, Bruce at Skelton, near Middlesbrough, Vesci at Malton and Mowbray at Thirsk.

Faced with such overwhelming odds, John was forced to concede and agreed to meet the barons at Runnymede on the banks of the River Thames to sign Magna Carta. A group of 25 leading noblemen formed a committee to oversee the drafting of Magna Carta and were principal witnesses to the signing. Eight of these were Northern nobles, including Richard de Percy, Robert de Ros, Eustace de Vesci, William de Mowbray and John de Lacy, Lord of Pontefract and Clitheroe and whose vast estates stretched as far as the boundaries of York and Selby.

Yet these Northern rebels didn't really prosper from the treaty, which was watered down by the Southern rebels, who sought compromise – the Northern rebels were in favour of deposing John and electing a new king. Within a year, John felt strong enough to march north and punish the rebels, fining the City of York £1,000 for backing the wrong side. But John was dead by the end of 1216 and Magna Carta was never overturned.

Millennium Press

Put it there, John!

Magna Carta

King John

A GREAT day for the civil liberties of every Englishman, was how a spokesman for the barons described today's historic ceremony at Runnymede on the banks of the River Thames.

King John's reluctant agreement to put his mark on the Magna Carta - or 'Great Charter' - signalled a blow to his desire to rule by royal whim and a great achievement for the barons, who have united to bring the king to heel and make him recognise the rule of law and the protection granted to every Englishman under that law.

King John's attempts to

Barons force King to sign their 'Great Charter'

rule without counsel and outside the laws of the land angered many of his subjects but the objections of the barons, especially the Northern ones, led to today's historic charter.

Leading opponents to the King's rule included Ros at Helmsley, Stuteville at Kirkbymoorside, Percy at Topcliffe, Vesci at Malton and Mowbray at Thirsk.

When the King agreed to talks and a committee of 25 barons was convened to draw up the charter, eight of them were from the North, including

Richard de Percy, Robert de Ros, Eustace de Vesci, William de Mowbray and John de Lacy, Lord of Pontefract and Clitheroe. They were witnesses and signatories at today's event.

Yet even before the ink is dry there are rumours that the King intends to ignore the charter.

And the Northern barons are angry that the final charter was 'watered down'. It is thought they favoured deposing the King and electing their own - a revolutionary idea!

The Battle of Boroughbridge
March 16, 1322

*T*HE beginning of the 14th century was a turbulent time for York and North Yorkshire and before the first quarter of the century was ended thousands of Yorkshiremen would lose their lives in bloody conflict.

The cause was the corrupt government of Edward II linked to the resurgence of Scottish nationalism. Edward's father, Edward I, had earned the name of the Hammer of the Scots, but the Scots were never truely subdued by him and the accession to the throne of Edward II – the first Prince of Wales – fuelled their nationalism.

Edward was a king of very little brain. He had little of his father's military acumen and he managed to alienate the whole country by his style of government – ignoring his usual advisers, the English nobles, and relying on a string of personal favourites, particularly Piers Gaveston.

Opposition built up, centred around Edward's cousin, Thomas of Lancaster, who was based at the former Lacy stronghold of Pontefract Castle, and supported by many local noblemen. In 1312, while Edward held his court in York, as his father had done, to be near the border with Scotland, the rebels besieged Scarborough Castle, seized Gaveston and summarily executed him.

Edward was powerless to take revenge and Thomas of Lancaster became virtual ruler of England. Edward was back in control two years later, however, just in time for the humiliating defeat at Bannockburn in 1314. Once again Edward found himself back in York – his first stop after fleeing the field.

Worse was to come. In 1319 Edward returned to York, gathered an army and marched north to besiege Berwick-upon-Tweed. While there, the Scots slipped past him and attacked York. The city held out but the suburbs were burned.

An indignant lord mayor, Nicholas Fleming, raised troops to pursue the Scots. He caught them at Myton-on-Swale but while the troops from York crossed the river, the Scots fell on them, butchering Fleming and 3-4,000 local men. Once again Edward returned to York.

This was all too much for Thomas of Lancaster and he again sought local support for a rebellion. He was joined by many leading noblemen, chiefly John, Lord Clifford; Roger, Lord Mowbray and Joceline d'Eivill.

The issue came to a head at Boroughbridge on March 16, 1322 when the king's forces and the rebels clashed. For once Edward's military skill – or rather that of his supporter, Sir Andrew Harclay – won the day. Harclay, Sheriff of Cumberland, had invented the hobelar – a lightly armed but mounted infantryman – and Cumberland and Westmorland hobelars proved too much for the men of North Yorkshire under Thomas of Lancaster. The rebels were defeated and their leaders captured.

Lancaster was taken back to his own castle at Pontefract and executed, while Mowbray, d'Eivill and Clifford were taken by river to York, where they were also tried and executed. Mowbray's body was left swinging in chains at the gallows for three years before being buried in Toft Green. Clifford suffered a more famous fate. After execution, his body was hung from the walls of the castle keep, an event that almost certainly led to it being named Clifford's Tower.

York's problems were not yet over. Later that same year Edward returned to York to gather troops for another foray against the Scots. They clashed near Byland Abbey and again the Scots were victorious, nearly capturing Edward himself. Once again the men of the county of York paid with their lives for Edward's military incompetence.

Millennium Press

March 16, 1322   **A thousand years of York's history**

King overcomes Yorkshire rebels

A victory at last for Edward as York pays

KING Edward II, vanquished at Bannockburn, outfoxed at Berwick-on-Tweed and outsmarted at Scarborough, finally got the military victory he sought - but at a terrible price for the men of York and North Yorkshire.

The victory of the King's forces over the Northern rebels, led by Thomas of Lancaster, at Boroughbridge today restored a little credibility to the King's tarnished military reputation, but at the expense of Northern troops who have suffered greatly of late at the hands of the Scots.

It is just three years since nearly 4,000 troops from

Rebel billmen prepare for the clash with the King's forces at Boroughbridge. The billmen proved no match for the 'hobelars' of Sir Andrew Harclay

York and North Yorkshire were slaughtered at Myton-on-Swale by the Scots after they had slipped past the King at Berwick and attacked York.

It was this event, coupled with the King's incompetence, both military and civil, that caused many local men to join the rebels.

For once, the King's military acumen won the day - or rather that of Sir

Andrew Harclay, Sheriff of Cumberland. His 'hobelars' proved invincible.

After the battle Thomas of Lancaster was returned to his castle at Pontefract for execution while other leaders were brought to York. It is believed that John, Lord Clifford, is destined to hang in chains from the walls of York's castle keep after his execution.

OUR CUSTOMERS HAVE LEARNED TO EXPECT UNCOMPROMISING QUALITY

THE PRINCIPLES OF AVIATION

In the demanding field of aviation, quality is not merely an option, it is a must. Each instrument must meet the highest safety and reliability criteria. In tune with this approach, we have constantly optimized the functions on each of our chronographs. The launch of the EMERGENCY, the first watch to feature a built-in micro-transmitter, constituted an unprecedented technological breakthrough. This genuine survival instrument is worn by military and civilian pilots around the world as well as by members of the major national flight teams. One simply does not become an aviation supplier by chance.

THE ESSENCE OF BREITLING

EMERGENCY. The wrist instrument worn by Bertrand Piccard and Brian Jones during their non-stop round-the-world balloon flight on BREITLING ORBITER 3.

Inglis & Son
(Jewellers) Ltd.
Established 1866

GOLDSMITHS · SILVERSMITHS · CUTLERS

AGENTS FOR THE WORLD'S MOST FAMOUS WATCHES & CLOCKS. DIAMOND, ENGAGEMENT, WEDDING & SIGNET RINGS.

52-54 Stonegate, York. YO1 8AS. Tel (01904) 654104

INSTRUMENTS FOR PROFESSIONALS
www.breitling.com

BREITLING
1884

The building of the Merchant Adventurers' Hall

1357 - 1361

*I*N these days of fast road and rail links, it is easy to forget that for centuries York was an important port. In medieval times, roads were dreadful and rivers were a much more practical means of transport. Before the building of Naburn weir and lock in the 18th century, the Ouse was tidal, with York the most upstream point sea-going cargo vessels could reach. Since Roman times, and possibly earlier, people had brought their goods downstream to York for sale and transfer to vessels heading for ports all over northern Europe as well as up and down the East Coast of England.

This brought great revenues to the city – revenues which were greatly increased when York was made a Staple town in 1352. Staple towns were those permitted by the king and Parliament to deal exclusively in certain commodities, such as wool, leather and lead. York's elevation to the ranks of the Staple towns made it sole purveyor of all the wool and leather goods produced in North Yorkshire – a massive amount thanks to the thriving monasteries in the Dales and Ryedale.

The benefits to York were immediate and long-lasting: several York men, including John Thrush of Hungate and two Lord Mayors of York, William Holbeck and Thomas Beverley, became Mayors of Calais Staple. Calais was an English possession and the main point of import in Continental Europe for English goods. The Mayor of Calais Staple was a vastly-influential (and rich) figure.

Closer to home, the elevation of the city to a Staple town produced a great dividend for a local guild. The Gild of Mercers (dealers in cloth) and Merchant Adventurers – now the Merchant Adventurers – had probably been in existence for some 200 years. Certainly there is mention in 1139 of a similar gild in existence in York and given York's prominence as a market it seems certain to have continued in existence down to the 14th century.

Emboldened by their new-found wealth, three York guild members, John Freebois, John Crome and Robert Smeton, bought four acres of land off Fossgate in 1356 and the following year the guild was granted a licence to incorporate. Later that year work started on its new guildhall. The Merchant Adventurers' Hall, still standing proud six centuries later, was finished in 1361 and is an outstanding example of a medieval guildhall.

The hall, added to at later dates, comprised a great hall, where members met to transact their business, an undercroft where the members established a charity hospital, and a chapel, where they prayed.

From the quays on the Foss outside the hall, ships sailed all over Europe, but especially to Calais. Another thriving trade was established with Ghent, which imported English wool for the skilled Flemish weavers. Ghent was once on the coast of what is now Belgium but when the North Sea began to silt up the Flemings built a canal from Ghent to the sea. Thus one of the most thriving import-export businesses of the Middle Ages was conducted between two ports miles from the sea!

Nowadays it's easy to think of York as a tourist haunt full of old buildings, with a little light industry and commerce. Because of the efforts of the Merchant Adventurers and their fellow guilds in the city, York was a thriving trading centre, on a par with modern giants like Manchester or Birmingham.

Millennium Press

Adventurers' great hall opens

The Merchant Adventurers' great hall on the banks of the River Foss

THE great new guildhall of the Gild of Mercers and Merchant Adventurers has finally opened to usher in what is hoped will be a new age of prosperity for York.

The splendid hall, off Fossgate and with a quay on the banks of the River Foss, has taken four years to complete. Using the latest technological advances of the 14th cen-

Gild hopes to bring prosperity to the city

tury, it comprises a great hall for gild members to conduct their business, a chapel and an undercroft which will house a charitable hospital.

From the hall gild members are expected to export wool and leather goods along the coast of Britain and to the Continent.

In particular, the trade in good English wool to the town of Ghent in the Low Countries is expected to benefit and prosper.

And this increased wealth is certain to benefit not only the gild and its members but the whole of York.

The execution of Archbishop Scrope
June 8, 1405

MANY famous heads have sat atop the bars of York, especially Micklegate - traitors of great and small rank, claimants to the throne, rebels and Scottish invaders. But only one Archbishop of York has earned the dubious 'privilege' of ending his days there.

Richard Scrope, son of Lord Scrope of Masham, was a seemingly honest and principled man who took exception to Henry IV's methods of government, stood up for his principles and fell victim to the devious machinations of the King and his supporters.

Henry IV was one of England's most unpopular kings. He was not the legal heir to the throne, seizing it by force and ruled badly before dying in great agony, possibly of leprosy. The first king of the House of Lancaster, his attempts to secure the throne for his dynasty led in great part to the Wars of The Roses.

Henry, formerly Henry Bolingbroke, Duke of Hereford, had been banished by his predecessor, Richard II, but while Richard was campaigning in Ireland, Henry landed in Yorkshire in 1399 and seized the throne. Richard was arrested on his return and held in various castles, including Leeds, Pickering and Knaresborough before being put to death in horrifying circumstances in Pontefract Castle.

Henry soon fell out with the men who had supported him, especially the powerful Percy family, refusing to pay them money owed and things came to a head at Shrewsbury in 1403, when Henry was victorious and Henry Percy (the Hotspur of Shakespeare) killed.

The Percies held much land in Yorkshire and their supporters were particularly resentful over Henry's actions afterwards, as the avaricious king attempted to obtain more and more taxes from his subjects while ignoring their civil liberties.

Yorkshire was a hotbed of discontent and things came to a head in 1405. Unfortunately Archbishop Scrope played his hand too early. Impatient for the rebellion to start, he prompted it by issuing a series of articles listing Henry's abuses. These were nailed on every church door in his diocese and he also sent them around the country. In the meantime he preached a seditious sermon in York Minster. It must have been some speech for 20,000 men responded to his call to arms.

Henry sent 30,000 men under the Earl of Westmorland. When they arrived in the city, they found Scrope's army drawn up near the present Shipton-by-Beningbrough in positions so powerful that Westmorland decided to talk rather than fight.

Westmorland simply tricked Scrope, promising him a friendly ear and persuading him to disband his army. As soon as this happened Scrope was seized and carried off to York.

His trial took place later that year in the great hall of Bishopthorpe Palace, with the King himself presiding. Thomas Arundel, Archbishop of Canterbury and former Archbishop of York, pleaded for Scrope's life and the Chief Justice of England, Gascoigne, refused to pass sentence on the disgraced Archbishop, claiming he had no jurisdiction over a clergyman, but Scrope was condemned anyway and on June 8, 1405 taken to a field close to where Southlands Methodist Chapel now stands where he was beheaded. His head was placed on Micklegate Bar and his body taken back to the Minster for burial.

Henry's revenge was short lived. It is said that on the very day Scrope was executed, the King was struck down with the leprosy which was to end his life eight years later.

Millennium Press

June 8, 1405   **A thousand years of York's history**

Archbishop of York executed!

Scrope is beheaded for act of treason

THE head of Richard Scrope, Archbishop of York, tonight sits atop Micklegate Bar, the first archbishop to join the ranks of traitors, false claimants and Scotsmen, who have previously adorned the main gateway to the city.

The archbishop met the headsman's axe today on a field at Southlands, just outside the city walls, sent to his death by King Henry IV himself, after Lord Chief Justice Gascoigne refused to pass sentence on Scrope - and after a futile plea for clemency from Thomas Arundel, Archbishop of Canterbury and a former

Micklegate Bar, where tonight Archbishop Richard Scrope's head sits after he was executed for treason

Archbishop of York.

Scrope's crime was to speak out against the King, although many would argue that his real crime was to trust Henry IV.

A thundering sermon against the King's excesses backed up by a series of articles listing Henry's 'crimes' resulted in 20,000 men taking up arms against Henry. But when Henry's commander, the Earl of Westmorland, promised a

parley, Scrope disbanded his army - only to be seized by Westmorland and dragged off to York for trial.

The trial was a foregone conclusion with Henry VI announcing the verdict of death by beheading.

It is rumoured however, that retribution won't be long coming as the King has reportedly contracted leprosy - the symptoms of which first showed themselves at the time of Scrope's execution.

The Battle of Towton
March 29, 1461

*M*ORE myths and misconceptions exist about the Wars of the Roses and the Battle of Towton than any other British conflict.

This was not a struggle between two northern counties – it was a dynastic struggle for the throne of England, complicated by anger at bad government and over-powerful nobles. It was not a continuous war lasting for 30 years but rather a series of battles interspersed with periods of uneasy peace. Even the names of the combatants are misleading. The House of York had little connection with York: its power base was in Kent, the Welsh Borders and the South West. And although the House of Lancaster had Lancastrian connections, its main power base was Yorkshire (York was a staunchly Lancastrian city).

The trouble stemmed from Henry IV's seizure of the throne from Richard II. Henry was not the legal claimant: that was Edmund, Earl of March. His descendants felt the throne should be theirs, especially as the present incumbent, Henry VI, grandson of Henry IV, was a weak and feeble-minded man more interested in church affairs than those of state. Richard, Duke of York, headed the Yorkist side, Margaret of Anjou, the strong-minded queen, headed the Lancastrian contingent, while Richard Neville, Earl of Warwick (the 'Kingmaker') flitted between the sides to advance his own family's interests.

In 1461, the Lancastrians were in the ascendancy. The previous year, a carefully laid trap had been sprung at Wakefield and the Duke of York and his young son, the Earl of Rutland, killed (the latter allegedly butchered after the battle by Lord Clifford).

Clifford's comeuppance was not long in coming.

The Yorkist cause was now carried by the able and daring new duke, Edward (later Edward IV). Early in 1461 he marched north to confront the Lancastrians, based at York, where the King and Queen had taken up residence – and where the heads of Edward's father (still wearing a paper crown) and brother rested on Micklegate Bar. The two sides met on Palm Sunday, 1461, between Towton and Saxton, near Tadcaster, with 1,000 volunteers from the City of York (whose total population was probably less than 15,000) swelling the Lancastrian forces to around 20,000. The Yorkists could muster only 18,000, some 5,000 of which, under the Duke of Norfolk, were delayed crossing the River Aire.

The Lancastrians arrived first and chose the best ground, a high plateau with Cock Beck on their right and a deep depression, up which the Yorkists would have to advance, in front of them. But two major blows struck them before the battle: Clifford, one of their ablest commanders, was killed in a skirmish and then, as the Yorkists drew up their battle lines, it started to snow – right into the Lancastrians' faces.

The Yorkist archers soon started to decimate the Lancastrians, whose own arrows, held up by the wind, fell short. The Yorkists picked up the fallen arrows and fired them back. Faced with staying put and dying under an arrow storm or abandoning their good position, the Lancastrians decided on attack and marched down the hill. Bloody hand-to-hand fighting ensued and for a while it looked as if the Lancastrians would win the day but the arrival of the Duke of Norfolk turned the tide and the Lancastrians fled.

Some 28,000 men died that day (Cock Beck and the Wharfe at Tadcaster supposedly ran red with blood) making it the bloodiest battle ever fought on English soil. How many of those 1,000 York volunteers returned to their homes is not known but given the scale of the slaughter, it would seem likely it was precious few.

Millennium Press

Slaughter of our troops at Towton

King's army shattered by Yorkist usurper

DISASTER struck the Royal cause at Towton, near Tadcaster, today, Palm Sunday, after his majesty, King Henry VI's forces were smashed by the troops of the Yorkist usurper, Edward, Duke of York, who styles himself King Edward IV.

The slaughter was great on both sides - perhaps as many as 28,000 men killed, the majority our loyal Lancastrian troops - and it is said that Cock Beck and the River Wharfe ran red with their blood.

Already military analysts are trying to understand what went wrong. The Lancastrian forces out-

The two sides clash at Towton. After a bitter struggle the Yorkists were victorious

numbered their opponents and arrived early enough to select the best ground.

The Royal forces were drawn up in a good defensive position on the high ground, forcing the Yorkists to advance up the hill.

However, it is believed that the Lancastrian tactics were thwarted by the weather. As the battle got under way, it began to snow - right into the faces of our men, who also found their

arrows falling short.

Even then victory might have been won had not more Yorkist troops arrived under the Duke of Norfolk.

The slaughter was great and it is not known how many of the 1,000 men of York who fought on the Royal side will return.

In the meantime King Henry VI and Queen Margaret have fled York, which now awaits the entrance of the conquering King Edward IV.

The re-consecration of York Minster

July 3, 1472

*T*HE superlatives are endless: the largest Gothic cathedral north of the Alps; England's largest Medieval building; York's crowning glory and a masterpiece in stone and glass. York Minster has earned all of these and the building we know now was finished and re-consecrated on July 3, 1472 at the conclusion of 250 years of rebuilding.

There has been a church on the Minster site (once the headquarters of the Roman legionary fortress at York) since 627AD when Edwin, the pagan King of Northumbria, converted to Christianity. The first church was built of wood and work started on a stone building to replace it before Edwin's death in 632. It was dedicated to St Peter and thus was born the Cathedral Church of St Peter or York Minster, although the Saxon word 'minster' refers to a church connected to a monastery and there is no record of there ever having been a monastery at the Minster.

The Saxons were not great builders in stone and only 40 years later the great St Wilfrid was complaining that the poor state of the roof was allowing water in, the glass was unglazed and birds were nesting in the building.

Fire destroyed this church in 741 (60 years after St Wilfrid's complaints) and a new church was built with rounded arches and panelled ceiling. This church was to last more than 300 years before perishing by fire in 1069. Norman soldiers, preparing to resist a siege by Danish invaders and Saxon rebels, fired a few Saxon hovels to clear a fighting space, the fire got out of control and the Minster went up in flames.

It lay in ruins for a few years, being sacked again by Danish raiders in 1075 before Thomas of Bayeux, the first Norman archbishop, decided to rebuild. The Norman Minster was an impressive building, 365 feet long and with walls seven feet thick. But it wasn't impressive enough for Walter de Grey, Archbishop of York from 1215 to 1255. He wanted a massive cathedral in the new gothic style sweeping the country. And in 1220 work started on the North and South Transepts, which were completed in 1250.

That was the start of a massive task. Over the next 220 years all the parts that make up the modern Minster were completed - but not without many trials and tribulations.

There were problems with staff: one master carpenter lost his head for heights and had to be replaced; a master mason was attacked by jealous colleagues and his assistant murdered; the Black Death killed many craftsmen, including a master mason, and squabbles and petty pilfering caused many hold-ups.

And the technical problems were immense: the original idea to have stone roof vaulting had to be abandoned and timber used (suitable timber was difficult to find); the problems of moving immense blocks of stone (quarried at Tadcaster, brought by river down the Wharfe and up the Ouse and then dragged up the street that now bears the name of 'Stonegate') were enormous and the simple pulleys and lifting gear of the time struggled to cope; and to cap it all the central tower partially collapsed in 1407.

Yet despite all these setbacks, the Minster was completed - in 1470 - and on July 3, 1472, Archbishop George Neville, brother of the Earl of Warwick (the 'Kingmaker') was able to re-consecrate the Minster, York's crowning glory and a fitting tribute to the dedication, passion and religious commitment of generations of York men and women.

Millennium Press

Unveiled: glories of our Minster

A 250-year tasks ends with special ceremony

ARCHBISHOP George Neville today conducted the re-consecration ceremony of York Minster - a ceremony which marked the culmination of a 250-year task.

York's cathedral church has undergone many rebuilds since the first wooden Minster was built in 627AD but none as spectacular or as glorious as the latest version.

The magnificent gothic church was the brainchild of Archbishop Walter de Grey, who decided to replace the Norman church.

Work started in 1220 and the first section, the rebuilding of the North

York Minster, bedecked with flowers to celebrate its re-consecration after a 250-year rebuilding scheme

and South Transepts, was completed in 1250.

It has taken another 222 years to complete the rest of the building - a period extended by a variety of problems, including disputes with the workers, the Black Death and technical problems which

were highlighted by the collapse of the central tower in 1407.

Now the largest cathedral north of the Alps and York's crowning glory, is complete - a tribute to the work and dedication of the citizens of York over the centuries.

Battle of Bosworth Field
August 22, 1485

THE penultimate battle of the Wars of the Roses (the Yorkists were to have one last, desperate fling at Stoke two years later) may have been fought in faraway Leicestershire but once again men of York took part - and once again, as at Towton 24 years earlier, they were on the losing side.

How they came to be fighting for the Yorkist cause at Bosworth when for most of the period of the Wars of the Roses the city was staunchly Lancastrian, is a fascinating story and one that revolves round England's most reviled king, Richard III.

The Tudors' chief propagandist, William Shakespeare, portrayed the younger brother of Edward IV as a hunchbacked monster who murdered his nephews (including the legal King), his brother and many of his rivals in his megalomaniac desire for the throne.

In the second half of this century the pendulum has swung the other way, with apologists trying to persuade us that Richard was something akin to a saint.

The truth, as always in these matters, lies somewhere between the two.

Richard was not a perfect physical specimen (contemporary reports mention one shoulder higher than the other, there's a portrait altered to apparently paint out a hump and a York schoolmaster, John Payntour, was fined for calling him 'crouchback'); he dealt with his opponents ruthlessly, executing two of Edward IV's brother-in-laws after a summary trial and having one of his greatest supporters, Lord Hastings, executed without trial. Named as Lord Protector after Edward IV's death, he deposed his young nephew Edward V and had him declared illegitimate and seized the throne.

On the plus side, he was a brave soldier (his physical deformity can't have been that great), a religious man and a patron of the arts (he encouraged William Caxton to set up his printing press and owned one of the finest private libraries in England at the time); was a more than capable administrator (he understood the problems of his time and his remedies were eagerly taken up by Henry VII) and seemed to be that rarity of the time - a loving husband and father.

But everyone seems to have been in agreement about one thing - he was an excellent leader of the Council of the North. Edward IV had created the council in 1472, basing it in York and making Richard - then Duke of Gloucester - its first head. The recent rebellion by the Earl of Warwick had seen all his lands confiscated and his northern realms were handed over to Richard. He based himself at Middleham Castle, where he married the love of his life, Anne Neville, but he spent much of his time on council business in York, where he gradually won over the citizens.

In the 11 years until Edward IV's death, Richard brought peace and prosperity to the city (although disgruntled Lancastrians in the county were less happy), so much so that when he marched to Bosworth to confront Henry Tudor, a body of troops from York marched with him - although it must be pointed out that only 80 men marched south compared with the 1,000 from the city who fought with the Lancastrians at Towton.

The result, aided by betrayal and treachery, was defeat for Richard and fear for the city. So famous throughout the land was their love for Richard, the city fathers waited for Henry's retribution. It never came. The first Tudor monarch assured the city he wouldn't punish them and offered a pardon to all the York men who fought at Bosworth - although six of them, including Miles Metcalfe, the City Recorder, had to wait three months for their pardon.

Millennium Press

Richard killed at Bosworth Field

York troops among army defeated by Henry Tudor

KING Richard III, former leader of the Council of the North in York, was today deposed by the Welsh usurper, Henry Tudor.

In a bloody battle at Bosworth Field in Leicestershire, Tudor's forces, aided by defections from the King's ranks, proved victorious.

The King is reported to have fought bravely but is thought to have perished in the battle. A search has been launched for his body, although his crown has been found in a thorn bush.

Richard's deeds as leader of the Council of the North, when he was Duke of Gloucester,

Richard III: killed at the Battle of Bosworth Field

endeared him to the citizens of this city - so much so that 80 of them marched off to Bosworth to fight on his side.

Richard had attracted some controversy of late, especially over his moves to declare his nephews illegitimate and seize the the throne himself, but after years of unrest many saw the move as vital for the wellbeing of

the Kingdom. After the horrors of the Wars of the Roses, the last thing the country needed was a boy king.

However, it is believed that some of the nobles were unhappy with Richard's plans to curtail their power and this may have forced them into the arms of Henry VII, as the new king is styling himself.

The Pilgrimage of Grace
October, 1536

*Y*ORK enjoyed nearly 1,500 years as one of the leading cities of the kingdom. From the day in AD71 when the Romans first established their legionary headquarters at the place with the rivers Ouse and Foss met, York was destined to play a major role in English affairs - as a garrison town during the long conflicts with the Scots, as a judicial and administrative centre, as a port, market and trading centre and even, on occasions, capital of England.

But after the death of Richard III at Bosworth Field in 1485, more and more power was settled in London and the South, and the North's pivotal role in English affairs was gradually reduced. Hopes were high that the change could be reversed but those hopes were finally dashed in 1536 by the Pilgrimage of Grace.

The trigger for the East Riding-based rebellion was Henry VIII's 1536 Dissolution of the Monasteries Act. Although this only affected the small religious houses (St Clement's Nunnery was the only York religious house to be closed) it was the beginning of the end for a way of life.

It was not just the threat to peoples' religious beliefs but to their livelihoods. Monasteries in the Middle Ages were great employers, hiring local men and women to serve as servants, cooks, gardeners, shepherds and fieldhands. Local economies in many areas were highly dependent on the monasteries and their closure brought much financial hardship.

In addition monasteries provided poor relief, ran hospitals and schools and even provided board and lodgings for weary travellers.

But the Pilgrimage of Grace was not just about religion and employment. The Tudors were the creators of modern Britain and one of the ways they dragged the country out of the Middle Ages was to centralise power in London. Powerful Northern magnates saw not only their wealth but also their power eroded. Amongst the most disgruntled in this area were the Percies and their tenants, based mainly in the old East Riding.

It was here that the Pilgrimage of Grace started. The leader was Robert Aske, a London lawyer, but from a prominent Beverley family. Amongst his supporters were two brothers of the Earl of Northumberland (who prudently steered clear of the rebellion), Sir Thomas Percy and Sir Ingram Percy.

Aske, an articulate and clever man, raised an army of 20,000 men and marched on York. Within a month his army had doubled in size and they set off for London. They were met by the King's forces, under the Duke of Norfolk, at Doncaster and when Norfolk saw the size of the opposing force, he decided to parley.

It was to prove fatal for the rebels. Aske, like Archbishop Scrope a century before, accepted the word of the King's lieutenant, only to be arrested once his forces had been disbanded.

Aske was tried in London but returned to York, where he was executed at Clifford's Tower. Hundreds went to the gallows around the county, including many Percy supporters, while John Pickering, prior of the Dominican Priory in Toft Green, along with the abbots of Fountains, Jervaux and Rievaulx and the Prior of Bridlington were hanged at London's Tyburn.

If York could take any comfort from the failure of the rebellion it was in its increased status when Henry reinstated the Council of the North - which had been disbanded after the death of Richard III - in the city.

Millennium Press

October, 1536 **A thousand years of York's history**

Pilgrimage fails: Aske is executed

King goes back on his word to protesters

LONDON lawyer Robert Aske, a member of the prominent East Riding family, has been hanged for his part in the so-called Pilgrimage of Grace.

Aske, the leader of the rebellion which had its roots in King Henry VIII's dissolution of the monasteries, met his end at Clifford's Tower, York, after being returned to the city from his trial in London.

Aske had raised some 20,000 men in the East Riding, and had gathered support from two prominent members of the Earl of Northumberland's family, Sir Thomas Percy and Sir Ingram Percy -

Clifford's Tower, York, where Robert Aske was executed today for his part in the 'Pilgrimage of Grace'

although we stress that the Earl had no connection with the rebellion.

Aske's army, which quickly doubled in size, set off for London, only to meet the king's representative, the Duke of Norfolk, at Doncaster. When the Duke offered the men the king's ear, Aske disbanded his army - only to be seized by the

King and sent for trial.

While Aske was returned to York, John Pickering, prior of the Dominican house in Toft Green, along with the abbots of Fountains, Jervaux and Rievaulx abbeys, have been sent to London for execution.

Other executions are expected to follow around the county.

The death of
Margaret Clitherow
March 25, 1586

W AS Margaret Clitherow, who was canonised in 1970, a true saint, who died for her religion, or the agent of a foreign power who sheltered the Queen's enemies? What is without doubt is that Margaret was a wife and mother, a devoted Catholic - and died a horrible death.

But her end came not because of her religion but because she broke a 300-year-old English law.

When Elizabeth I became England's second Protestant monarch in 1558, she promised a measure of religious tolerance for her subjects. "I have no wish to make a window into men's souls," she said. Elizabeth offered her Catholic subjects the chance to follow their conscience - provided that made some attempt to pay lip service to the Protestant religion and didn't flaunt their Catholicism.

Elizabeth did pass laws to make church attendance compulsory, but, ever the grasping Tudor, she preferred to fine rich men and ignore the poorer recusants. Things gradually changed, however. Catholic Europe plotted to overthrow Protestant England and fear of foreign invasion was rife. The founding of a college for Jesuit priests in Douai, in northern France, by a former canon of York Minster, William Allen, added a new twist. The trained priests were smuggled into England, ostensibly to minister to secret Catholic adherents, but also as agents of Philip of Spain, who was preparing to invade England.

Jesuit priests provided valuable information for Philip and were involved in several plots against Elizabeth. These agents provocateur were a dangerous threat to the country and harbouring them became an offence of high treason.

Margaret Clitherow (alternatively Clitheroe and Clithero) was born in 1556 in Davygate, the daughter of York wax chandler and one-time Sheriff, Thomas Middleton, and baptised at St Martin-le-Grand Church in Coney Street. In 1571 she married John Clitherow, a prosperous butcher and moved into his house in Shambles (although almost certainly not the house now dedicated as a shrine to St Margaret - her home was probably on the other side of the street).

Margaret was a devout Catholic, unlike her husband, and soon was in trouble with the law. She was fined several times and had three spells in prison for failing to attend church but couldn't deny her faith. It appeared to be fairly common knowledge in York that Mrs Clitherow was running a Catholic school in her house for her own four children and those of a neighbour, but the decision to harbour the Douai priests moved her from being a religious rebel to the rank of traitor.

Finally, the authorities raided her house, and although the priests hiding there were able to flee, a large quantity of incriminating evidence was found there. Margaret was taken to the Guildhall and charged with high treason. To spare her family and protect the fleeing priests, she refused to plead and was sent to the tollbooth prison on Ouse Bridge be pressed - literally under stones placed on a door over her. This had been the punishment since 1275 for those who refused to plead to any charge of a felony and from where we get the saying 'I must press you for an answer'.

There are examples of pressed men lasting up to 40 days, but poor Margaret, stripped almost naked, with her arms tied out at her side and with a small rock placed under the small of her back, lasted just 15 minutes, uttering only "Jesu, Jesu, Jesu, have mercy on me" before the life was crushed out of her.

She was not alone. By 1592, when the threat from Spain was over, 26 Catholic priests and 15 citizens of York had been executed, and Catholics were to live in fear for many years to come.

Millennium Press

Tragic death of York woman

Catholic rebel dies while being pressed

A prominent York Catholic, Mrs Margaret Clitherow, has died in Ouse Bridge's Tollbooth prison on the eve of her trial for treason.

Mrs Clitherow, wife of leading Shambles butcher, John Clitherow, died of pressing after she refused to plead to a charge of high treason.

In accordance with the 300-year-old law pertaining to felons who refuse to plead, she was pressed to plead but lasted only 15 minutes under the stone-laden door before expiring.

Mrs Clitherow was well known in the city for her Catholic faith and the city magistrates had cause to

York Catholic Margaret Clitherow: died today of pressing after refusing to plead to a charge of high treason

fine her on several occasions and imprison her three times.

It was widely believed she was holding a Catholic school in her house but when rumours started that she was hiding two

agents of Spain, authorities decided to raid the house. The Jesuit priests had fled but enough incriminating evidence was found to lodge a charge of high treason against the York woman.

The execution of Guy Fawkes
January 31, 1606

*H*E was a traitor, servant of a foreign and hostile power and a failed terrorist - yet Guy Fawkes is, without doubt, York's most famous son.

The story of the son of a leading city Protestant who became a Catholic soldier for the King of Spain and the most notorious terrorist in English history, is a fascinating one. What emerges is the story of a man brave and resolute yet easily led into a plot that couldn't really succeed and an action that gravely worsened the position of the Catholics in England.

Fawkes was born in York in 1570 and baptised in St Michael-le-Belfrey church. His parents were Edith, daughter of a rich York merchant, and Edward, a notary in the ecclesiastical courts. They lived in a house off Stonegate.

But despite being born into a family very much part of the Protestant establishment in York, Fawkes was to undergo a dramatic change in personal circumstances which was to eventually lead him to the scaffold.

In 1579 Fawkes's father died and his mother married again in 1583. Her new husband was Dennis Bainbridge, of Scotton Hall near Knaresborough. Scotton was a hotbed of Catholicism and Bainbridge an ardent Catholic with his own secret chapel. Faced with such influences - and no doubt affected by his schooling at St Peter's School in York, which was also rumoured to be rooted in the Catholic faith - Fawkes became a Catholic.

It was a brave - or foolish - move. In the later half of the 16th century, England was not a good place to be a Catholic. Elizabeth I's early tolerance and decision to turn a blind eye to her Catholic subjects, was giving way to suspicion and hatred, and numerous plots to overthrow Elizabeth and the threat of foreign invasion turned Catholic subjects from religious rebels to potential traitors.

Although the defeat of the Armada in 1588 removed the imminent threat of foreign invasion, England was a seething hotbed of resentment against its Catholic subjects and many were removed from office, fined or executed as the century grew to a close.

Fawkes avoided this by quitting England and joining the Spanish army in its campaign to subdue the Protestant Netherlands. Here he earned a reputation for bravery - and a knowledge of explosives.

Fawkes already had more than a passing acquaintance with several of the leading Gunpowder Plotters: John and Christopher Wright were fellow St Peterites; Thomas Winter and Thomas Percy were visitors to Scotton.

The plan was simple: dig a tunnel under the Houses of Parliament, fill it with gunpowder and set it off as the Protestant King James I attended the state opening of Parliament on November 5, 1605.

An explosives expert was needed and Fawkes's name cropped up. He was persuaded to take up the dangerous part of the plot, and when the plotters managed to hire a room under the chamber where the opening was to take place, Fawkes arranged for barrels of gunpowder to be placed there.

However, things quickly began to go wrong. Leading conspirator Robert Catesby recruited wealthy and prominent Catholics to the cause. These, unwilling to see friends die, relayed news of the plot to the Government, who set about rounding up the traitors. Fawkes was arrested skulking around the House and although he endured many days of dreadful torture, steadfastly stuck to his cover story in order to give his friends time to escape. It was all in vain. The Government was well aware of the conspiracy and quickly rounded up and executed the plotters. Fawkes, a broken man, went to his death in the Old Palace Yard, Westminster on January 31, 1606, too weak from his tortures to mount the scaffold unaided.

Millennium Press

Guy Fawkes executed!

Gunpowder plotter pays the ultimate penalty

Guy Fawkes: York man was executed today

YORK-BORN Guy Fawkes today paid the ultimate penalty for his treason when he was hanged, drawn and quartered in the Old Palace Yard at Westminster.

The former St Peter's schoolboy, who was baptised at St Michael-le-Belfrey church in York and grew up in Stonegate before moving to Scotton, near Knaresborough, was caught red-handed setting up a massive explosive charge under the Houses of Parliament. Fawkes intended to detonate the charge when His Majesty King James I opened Parliament.

Thankfully the plot was discovered in the nick of time and although Fawkes refused to name his co-conspirators, even under torture, all the plotters have been rounded up and received their just deserts.

Fawkes, born into a prominent York Protestant family, had been heading for a nasty end from early days.

It was believed that he converted to Roman Catholicism during his time at St Peter's and when he left school he left the country to serve in the army of the King of Spain, where he learnt about explosives.

On his return to England he quickly threw in his lot with the plotters.

Millennium Press

The Battle of Marston Moor and the Siege of York
1644

THE City of York played a prominent part in the English Civil War - and was to pay a heavy penalty for its support of King Charles I. The Civil War was a long time brewing as the King and Parliament disputed the right to rule. Things came to a head in 1642 when Charles quit the Parliamentary stronghold of London and moved his court to York. He set up residence in Minster Yard. From York he marched to Hull to seize the city's armoury but was refused admittance by the governor, Sir John Hotham. An infuriated Charles withdrew to York and attempted to summon Parliament in the city. When this move failed, he marched to Nottingham to raise his standard and set the Civil War in motion.

York remained a Royalist stronghold and when local volunteers were joined by 6,000 men under the Earl of Newcastle, became a heavily defended garrison town. The city's defences were strengthened, cannon mounted at strategic points and roads blocked with tubs of earth. Meanwhile, elsewhere the Royalist and Parliamentary forces had fought each other to a virtual standstill. The stalemate was to be broken in dramatic fashion at the beginning of 1644 when the Scots entered the war on the side of Parliament. A large Scottish army, under the Earl of Leven, headed south for York. Already Ferdinando, Lord Fairfax and his son, Sir Thomas, who had local links with Bilton and Nun Appleton, had imposed a partial blockade at Tadcaster and Wetherby.

The two sides first clashed at Selby, where the Royalists were defeated. Soon the Parliamentarians had York surrounded: the Scots set up a line from the York waterworks site near Leeman Road, across Acomb and Knavesmire to the Ouse at Middlethorpe; Sir Thomas Fairfax's men held ground from Fulford, over Garrowby Hill and through Tang Hall to the Foss at Yearsley Bridge; the third section to the Ouse at Clifton was held by a third parliamentary force under the Earl of Manchester and a rising star of the Parliamentary side, Oliver Cromwell.

The city began to take a real pounding from the Parliamentarian guns, while mines under Walmgate Bar and St Mary's Tower, at the junction of Marygate and Bootham, caused severe damage. After the latter explosion, Parliamentary forces broke through the ancient walls of St Mary's Abbey and succeeded in capturing the King's Manor before being driven off with heavy loss of life.

Finally a relieving army under Prince Rupert, the King's nephew, arrived and the Parliamentary forces withdrew to Marston Moor, four miles west of York. Prince Rupert, ignoring advice to exercise caution, marched out to meet the enemy. He had around 18,000 men; Parliament about 28,000.

They met on July 2, although action was in short supply as Rupert waited for the York garrison forces to join him. When they arrived at 4pm, the Royalists decided it was too late to fight that day. The Parliamentarians had other ideas and at 7pm, as Prince Rupert was enjoying his supper, they ordered the advance, forcing the Royalist forces into desperate action. For a while it was a close run thing but the numerical superiority and better discipline of the Parliamentarian forces eventually won the day and sounded the death knell for the Royalist cause. Some 5,000 men, two-thirds of them Royalist, lay dead on the battlefield.

Rupert marched away south, Newcastle fled to Scarborough and took ship to the Continent. It was left to the defenders of the city to strike the best personal terms they could. The Parliamentarians proved generous in victory and the garrison marched away leaving the city open to the Parliamentarian troops. They treated it relatively gently and at least the citizens' sufferings were over - as was York's part in the Royalist cause.

Millennium Press

July 2, 1644   A thousand years of York's history

Parliamentarians victorious

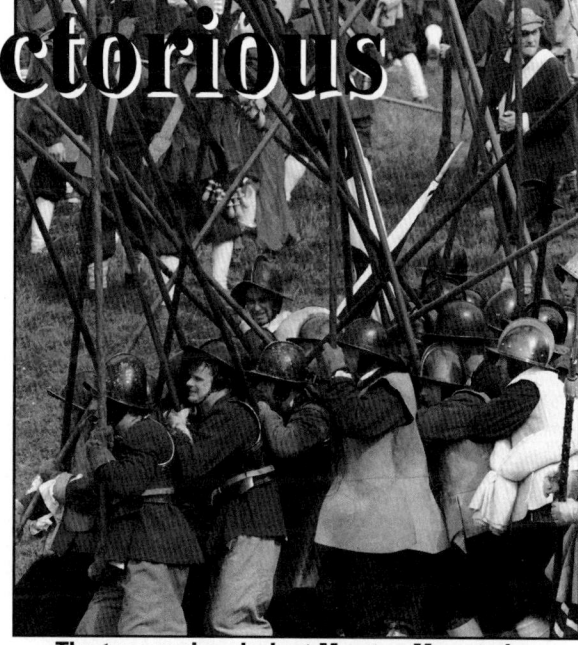

The two armies clash at Marston Moor today. Victory went to the forces of Parliament, leaving the King's army scattered and York at the mercy of the victors

King's army scattered at Marston Moor

THE future of the City of York looks bleak after a relieving army under Prince Rupert was smashed today at Marston Moor by the Parliamentary forces.

The siege of the city, which started at the beginning of this year, was expected to be lifted by the King's relieving army. But after a brief but bloody battle, the Parliamentarian forces, including a large contingent of Scots, was victorious.

It is believed that the Royal troops were caught unawares. It is reported that Prince Rupert, of the opinion that it was too late in the day for a battle, was actually taking his supper when the enemy attacked.

It is believed that more than 5,000 men fell in the battle, two thirds of them Royalist soldiers, including, no doubt, local men as a large contingent from the York Garrison fought on the Prince's side.

With the Prince marching south to join the King and the Earl of Newcastle heading for the Continent, York is virtually defenceless and will be forced to seek terms with the victors.

The opening of York Waterworks
1682

Y ORK, built on two rivers, has never been short of water. For generations citizens learned to go with the flow of Rivers Ouse and Foss. In medieval days, the Ouse was used as a highway, fishery, sewer and waste dump. It was also a ready supply of drinking water and a raw ingredient for brewers and bakers.

Although efforts were made to try to clean up York's rivers – the city authorities banned butchers from throwing animal refuse into the Ouse in 1377 – the first attempt to control York's water supply came in 1616. That year saw a Mr Maltby begin to lay pipes. To help his progress, he was permitted to take "certayn rough stones lyeing nere the Comon Hall as are not cerviceable for the Citties works," the city minutes reveal. As he laid more wooden pipes over Ouse Bridge, the Corporation decided to take a quarter share in the new waterworks.

But this system ultimately proved unsatisfactory, for in 1674 the Corporation consulted London merchant Henry Whistler about conveying water to the city. Three years later, Whistler entered into a covenant with the city to operate waterworks from St Leonard's Tower by the River Ouse. This tower, built as a fortification along the city walls, was no longer needed as a defence. He was instructed to "lay pipes, wheels and other engines and things necessary and convenient... for the drawing and conveying of water".

The first York Waterworks consisted of a single pump placed at the base of the tower and worked first by a windmill and later by two horses. In 1682 this began to "force water through wooden pipes into every street of the city, to the great convenience of the inhabitants," in the words of York historian Francis Drake.

Before iron pipes were used, water was conducted through bored-out elm trees. One end was coned so it could fit into the next pipe. Taps were fitted along the length to give citizens easy access to water when fire broke out.

The creation of York Waterworks appeared to bear out one of Knaresborough's Mother Shipton's predictions. The 15th century prophet was reported to have said: "Water shall come over Ouse Bridge, and a windmill shall be on a tower, and a'elm tree shall lie at every man's door."

In the middle of the 18th century, Colonel Thornton bought the works. He and his son brought in many improvements. A steam engine pump was added, along with hot and cold public baths in the house next to the tower – the only ones in the city. In 1779 the Waterworks were sold to a group of businessmen for £7,000. They installed a steam engine created by the designer of the Eddystone Lighthouse, John Smeaton.

One half of the city was supplied for two hours on Mondays, Wednesdays and Saturdays and the other half on Tuesdays, Thursdays and Fridays. No one saw a drop on Sundays. About 1,700 families took the service. Extra efforts were made on race weeks and for the meetings of the Assizes. Water was sold from carts straight from the Ouse at one penny per bucket.

By the mid-19th century the population of York outgrew the ability of the works to provide a proper supply. A company was formed in 1846, endorsed in Parliament by the York New Waterworks Act. The firm constructed the Acomb Landing treatment facility, taking water from the River Ouse just upstream of city pollution.

Pioneering filtering and treatment facilities were developed, including slow sand filtration, and in 1850, the York Waterworks began supplying a million gallons of fresh, clean water every day to the people of York. This saw the threat of cholera and other deadly water-borne diseases greatly diminished.

Millennium Press

1682   **A thousand years of York's history**

Clean water for the City of York!

Company will supply water through wooden pipes

A NEW water system, to replace the ill-fated 1616 scheme, will bring clean water to the City of York.

Mr Henry Whistler, of London, is to operate the York Waterworks company from St Leonard's Tower by the River Ouse.

He has installed a wind-driven pump at the base of the tower to draw water and pump it through a series of wooden pipes his men have been laying in the city these past few months.

The pipes, made from hollowed-out elm trees, have been laid in city streets and taps attached to the pipes so that citizens may draw water when needed. It is

St Leonard's Tower, the home of the new York Waterworks company

thought that the system will be particularly useful for fighting fires.

The main advantage, however, should be the supply of clean water to

the citizens - although the city council will need to be diligent over the quality of the Ouse water and ensure that no pollution of the waters occurs.

York's first newspaper, the York Mercury
February 23, 1719

*Y*ORK'S first newspaper contained no York news. But it was published by a local woman, Grace White. She was the second wife of printer John White. When he died, aged 80, in 1715 he left the business to Grace and his grandson, Charles Bourne.

As Charles was a minor, she carried on the business in her sole name. And on February 23, 1719, she and businessman Thomas Hammond published the first edition of the York Mercury.

It did not look anything like a modern newspaper. Surviving copies bound in York library show the page size was more akin to a small book than a broadsheet or tabloid newspaper. The titlepiece stated: "York Mercury: Or a General View of the Affairs of Europe, But more particularly Great-Britain: with Useful Observations on Trade. To be continued weekly. Price three pence."

It was on sale in "York; Whitby; Scarborough; Stoxley; Thirsk; North-Allerton; Hull; Malton; Beverley; Darlington; Bernard Castle; Easingwold; Rippon; Richmond; Stockton; Kirby; Pocklington; Selby; Skipton; Burrowbridge; Howden; Castleton; Yarm; Hunmanby; Glaisdale; Knarsborough; Settle; Preston. At all which places advertisements are taken in at two Shillings each."

The Mercury was printed weekly in Coffee Yard, Stonegate, and consisted entirely of extracts from the London papers. Items were reprinted from the British Journal, the St James Evening Post and the News Journal. New poems were published, and speeches from MPs, peers and other worthies reproduced in their entirety.

The copies in the reference library, dated between 1722 and 1724, cover such subjects as the South Sea Company, riots in Devonshire and the problem of pirates.

They also include items familiar to modern newspaper readers, such as the opinionated columnist. This is an extract from a piece attributed only to 'Criton', published in the York Mercury of May 23, 1724.

"I am sorry to see women so grossly treated by the men in so many places, and often by their own fault and consent. Men talk, and women hear such language as shocks all decency and tender ears. I know not which are most to blame; the men for their licentious and impure expressions or the women for hearing them with patience.

"It is more than probable that were they everywhere detested, they would be everywhere forborne. But while women will be entertained with foul ribaldry, or bear it without resentment, it will always be the theme of such men as know not how to be entertaining upon any other: and that by smutty hints and stories and double meanings, they can furnish them with words and make the women listen or smile and so grow filthy to make themselves agreeable."

There was also room for sensationalism, not to say invasion of privacy, in the Mercury. In one edition a private letter written by an "unfortunate young lady a little before she died", was published. "We know nothing of the lady's history," the paper said, "therefore cannot say whether her death was owing to the cruelty of her parents or the perfidiousness of her lover."

The letter concluded: "Yet this melancholy fate, sad and almost intolerable as it is, will not put an end to a life wholly miserable; but like gnawing vultures, preys on my health and strength and by degrees robs me of those blessings which I once possess'd in a very large manner."

In 1721 the York Mercury was taken over by Charles Bourne who continued it until his death in 1724. He was succeeded by Thomas Gent who changed the name to the "Original York Journal or Weekly Courant".

Millennium Press

A 'news-paper' is launched in York

'Mercury' is brainchild of York woman printer

YORK has its first 'news-paper'. The York Mercury, published today by Mrs Grace White, at a cost of three-pence, is the first such paper to be printed in York and contains a lively mixture of extracts from the London papers, poems, MPs' speeches plus a substantial number of advertisements from merchants through North Yorkshire and Teesside.

Mrs White, widow of York printer John White, operates a printing press out of Coffee Yard, off Stonegate, York.

She has gone into partnership with York businessman Mr Thomas Hammond to produce the Mercury, which Mrs White hopes will give: "A General View of the Affairs of Europe. But more particularly Great-Britain: with Useful Observations on Trade." The newspaper is to be published weekly and will circulate in, amongst other places, York, Whitby, Scarborough, Darlington, Ripon, Boroughbridge, Skipton, Howden, Selby and Preston.

Advertisements will cost two shillings each.

Coffee Yard, off Stonegate, York: the home of the city's first 'news-paper'

Racing begins on Knavesmire
1731

MEN have been racing horses in York for hundreds of years. In the third century, the Romans imported the finest Arab steeds into Eboracum to provide top quality sport. Patricians would assert their prestige by lending their names to races. These contests were highly competitive and may well have taken place on Knavesmire.

No record exists of racing again until the 16th century, when it was undertaken in the Forest of Galtres on the edge of York. Entrants competed to win the Lord Mayor's silver bell. The winning horse wore the bell on its headgear, until it was returned ready for the following year's race.

But the forest wasn't truly suited to the sport of kings and the authorities were on the lookout for a more suitable venue.

The problem was finding a long enough stretch of solid ground. York was surrounded by marshland, where the going was considerably more than soft.

So any large stretch of hard ground was likely to be tried out by the racing fraternity. In the bitterly cold winter of 1607, the frozen River Ouse became the venue for a whole series of sports. The climax of these improvised games was a horse race that started from Marygate Tower, went under the old Ouse Bridge and finished at Skeldergate Postern. Huge crowds gathered to watch the icy spectacle.

Later in the same century racing was held on Acomb Moor. Records show how King Charles I came to his "beloved citie of York" in 1633 and took in a meeting here. Incredibly, he was the last reigning sovereign to visit York races until Elizabeth II in 1972.

By the 1700s, another venue was being tried, Clifton Ings. Interest in the sport was growing and His Majesty's 100 Guineas was run as the opening race in the August meeting for many years.

But the Ings too was proving unsatisfactory. After persistent flooding postponed a meeting, it was decided to try Knavesmire.

At first glance, this seemed another unfortunate choice. As its name suggests, Knavesmire was a soggy bog. Its fame – or rather its notoriety – came from its role as the place of execution for York's criminals.

One man can be credited with creating a permanent racecourse on such unpromising foundations. York gardener John Telford used skill and dedication to level the land, drain it and prepare it for sport.

Six races were held at the inaugural meeting in 1731. Each consisted of heats and took an afternoon to compete. Knavesmire's first trophy winner was Monkey, a bay owned by Lord Lonsdale which won His Majesty's 100 Guineas. Two hundred years later the fifth Lord Lonsdale was racing his filly Myrobella at York.

Each subsequent day of the meeting had a theme: day two was for veteran horses; day three was for six-year-olds; day four was ladies' day; day five was the Galloway Plate and day six was for gentleman riders.

A surviving race card from 1733 shows that the names of runners were just as colourful then as they are today. They included: Hum Drum; Coney Skins; Quite Cuddy; Jack of the Green; Poor Robin; Vixen; and Creeper.

The races were an immediate hit among the northern nobility. The August meeting in particular was a major social event. It immediately followed the Assizes, where the judges would organise their own Knavesmire entertainment – public hangings.

In the evenings high society would remove to the Assembly Rooms, built in 1730. There, they would dance the night away at a colourful ball.

Millennium Press

Monkey does the business!

Lonsdale's horse is first winner on Knavesmire

MONKEY, a bay horse owned by Lord Lonsdale, was the first winner on York's new racecourse on Knavesmire.

The course, laid out by top York gardener, Mr John Telford, was in top condition and a large crowd enjoyed a splendid day's racing.

Six races, with corresponding heats, were held, and exciting sport was witnessed, with Lord Lonsdale's horse taking His Majesty's 100 Guineas.

After recent disappointments with various venues around the city, especially Clifton Ings, which was

Racegoers enjoy a night on the town at a grand Georgian Ball in York's Assembly Rooms to celebrate the first day's racing on Knavesmire

badly affected by flooding, the new course was hailed a great success.

After today's inaugural meeting, further days are to be devoted to veteran horses, six-year-olds, races for gentlemen riders, a

Galloway Plate Day and a Ladies' Day.

The racecourse committee are hoping to make the Knavesmire meetings a regular event and a major part of York's social calendar.

The Execution of Dick Turpin
April 7, 1739

*H*E was a vicious thug, poacher and horse stealer with a pock-marked face and a ready temper; he never owned a horse called Black Bess and he never made his famous ride from London to York. Yet the myth of Dick Turpin continues to grow as the truth is replaced by romantic fiction.

Born in Hempstead in Essex in 1705, the real Richard Turpin was the son of an inn-keeper and butcher who followed his father's latter trade. It was when he set himself up as a butcher that Turpin turned to a life of crime. He started buying poached game from a gang led by Samuel Gregory and the two soon abandoned the poaching game to form a large gang which preyed on isolated country households.

The gang, often up to 15 strong, would raid the homes of the rich, at first acting in a polite manner but soon resorting to increasing violence. One houseowner was held over a burning stove and badly burned and at another house a maidservant was raped. When three members of the gang were captured and one informed on them the gang split up. Turpin joined up with Thomas Rawdon and the pair became highwaymen until Turpin decided to lay low for a while and fled to Holland.

When he returned he teamed up with another highwayman, Matthew King, but when the latter was shot during an ambush (supposedly accidentally by his partner in crime) Turpin again fled - although not before he had shot and killed a witness.

This time he headed north (although not in a single day, a feat performed by another highwayman, John Nevison). Turpin instead headed for Brough, setting himself up as a horse trader named John Palmer.

It wasn't long before he was back to his old ways, this time dealing in stolen horses, but it was his famous temper which led to his downfall. When a neighbour's cockerel annoyed him, Turpin shot it and when a passer-by admonished him, threatened to murder the man.

Turpin (alias Palmer) was arrested and when he failed to come up with the bail money, remanded in custody. Soon his nefarious horse trading activities came to light and Turpin was transferred to York. In the meantime he had written to his brother-in-law in Hempstead asking for bail money but the man refused to pay the postage on the letter and the local postmaster, James Smith, recognised the handwriting as Turpin's.

Smith travelled to York to identify the highwayman and Turpin's fate was sealed. In the end he was never tried for the majority of his crimes. He was found guilty of two charges of horse stealing - a capital crime - and sentenced to hang.

After a couple of weeks in York's debtors' prison (now part of the Castle Museum) he was taken by cart through the city to York's Tyburn on Knavesmire, where he met his end bravely - although it took him five minutes to die.

The story doesn't end there. His body was put on view in the Blue Boar tavern in Castlegate but stolen by bodysnatchers that night. A hue and cry ensued and the mob finally rescued the body of a man who had become their hero.

Turpin was eventually buried in St George's churchyard, his body covered in quicklime to thwart the 'resurrection men.'

Then the rumours began. Within days stories of Turpin's life and crimes - almost wholly fictitious - were circulating in London.

But it was the novel, Rookwood, by Harrison Ainsworth, published a century later, that created the mythical figure of the dashing highwayman and wiped away the memories of a vicious thug who met a fitting end.

Millennium Press

April 7, 1739   **A thousand years of York's history**

Turpin hanged

Notorious highwayman ends his days at Tyburn

NOTORIOUS highwayman, housebreaker, murderer and horse stealer Dick Turpin, was hanged today on Knavesmire at York's 'three-legged mare' the Tyburn gallows.

The Essex-born Turpin, a former butcher who turned to house breaking and then highway robbery, went to his death bravely.

Taken from his cell at York Castle, Turpin joked with the crowd and waved gaily on his procession through the city to the gallows at Knavesmire.

His leg trembled slightly as he mounted the gallows' steps but he quickly regained his composure, facing the hanging bravely. He took five minutes to die.

So ended the career of one of Britain's most notorious characters. So great

Notorious highwayman Dick Turpin contemplates his fate before his execution on Knavesmire

was the manhunt for the man in the south east, that Turpin was forced to flee north to Brough, where he was living under the assumed name of John Palmer.

However when he shot a his neighbour's cockerel in a fit of temper and was subsequently arrested, Turpin's real identity was discovered and he was transferred

to York for trial.

While awaiting trial, the authorities discovered that Turpin couldn't keep away from a life of crime and had been organising horse stealing at his new base in the East Riding.

It was on this charge, rather than highway robbery or housebreaking, that he was tried, found guilty and sent for execution.

The Trials of the Jacobite Prisoners after Culloden
1746

T HE WINDSWEPT, heather-clad plain of Culloden Moor may seem a long way away from the green lawn of the Eye of York but there was a direct connection in 1746. Culloden was the battle that finally ended the Scottish Stuart claim to the British throne and secured the line of the German Hanoverians, but the rising of the clans in support of the Young Pretender, Charles Edward Stuart, 'Bonnie Prince Charlie' the previous year had almost toppled the monarchy.

The Prince's march south had taken him as far as Derby, but with the government in panic and George II reputedly packing his bags for a return to Hanover, the Prince turned back. His Highlanders - far from disciplined troops - were homesick and despite a string of easy victories were worried about their homes and families back in Scotland. So with the ultimate prize seemingly in his grasp, Charles turned back to Scotland, pursued by a large English army under the Duke of Cumberland, George II's second son, and met his nemesis on April 16, 1746 at Culloden, the windy height above the city of Inverness.

Here an English army aided by good discipline, excellent artillery, Hessian troops from Germany and, ironically, more Scotsmen than fought on Bonnie Prince Charlie's side, slaughtered the pride of the Highland clans and their Irish allies. Charles's and the Stuarts' dream died that day, and the aftermath was the end of a way of life that had endured for centuries.

The Duke of Cumberland spent three months mopping up the last Jacobite opposition, before heading south for a triumphant return to the capital. He was in York on July 25, when he dined with civic and church dignitaries before heading off for London at midnight. In the wake of the Royal entourage was a much more unenlightening sight - a row of Scottish prisoners. The government, still worried about the extent of Stuart support in Scotland, decreed that all rebels were to be tried in England, where they were less likely to gain a sympathetic hearing.

The important prisoners went to London but most of the rest were divided between Carlisle, Lancaster and York. The York prisoners were held in appalling conditions in cells that now form part of the Castle Museum. Here young and old, rich and poor Highlanders, many speaking no English, waited three months for justice. Surprisingly they received it. Some 75 prisoners eventually stood trial between October 2 and November 15, 1746 - and five were acquitted, amongst them John Ballantine of the Atholl Brigade, who successfully pleaded that he was pressed into service. The delighted Ballantine threw his bonnet into the air, crying: "Not guilty! Not guilty! Not guilty!" Of the remaining 70 condemned men, all sentenced to death, 47 or 48 (sources vary) had their sentences reduced to transportation for life to the Colonies or enlistment in the British Army.

The rest were hanged on a scaffold just a few yards from their cells.

There is some debate over the last to hang. CB Knight says it was James Mayne and William Connolly, whose heads were placed on Micklegate Bar, where they stayed for seven years before being stolen and secretly buried by William Arundel, a York tailor and Catholic, who received two year's imprisonment for his pains. Noted Scottish historian John Prebble, however, who claims 23 executions to Knight's 22, says the last to hang was James Reid of Angus, piper to Lord Ogilvy. The jury had recommended mercy as Reid had never carried arms or struck a blow but Lord Chief Baron Parker reminded them that "no regiment ever marched without musical instruments ... and therefore his bagpipes, in the eyes of the law, is an instrument of war." Reid was duly hanged.

Millennium Press

Scottish rebels condemned

York trials see 70 sent to the gallows

SEVENTY of the Jacobite prisoners captured at or soon after the Battle of Culloden, have been sentenced to death at York Assizes.

The trials, conducted by the Lord Chief Justice, Baron Parker, saw 75 Scottish prisoners facing the court for their part in the uprising against His Majesty, King George II. Most were captured at the Battle of Culloden, a glorious victory for his majesty's second son, the Duke of Cumberland on April 16 this year.

With feelings for the Stuart pretender still running high in Scotland, it was felt that all trials

A Scottish prisoner awaits his fate in a York prison cell after the victory of His Majesty's forces over the rebels at Culloden, near Inverness

should take place in England and Carlisle, Lancaster and York were earmarked for assizes, with the most important prisoners being taken straight to London.

The York jury showed its fairmindness by acquit-

ting five of the rebels. The rest were sentenced to death, although it is believed that most of them will be offered their lives in exchange for transportation to the colonies or enlistment in the British Army.

Laurence Sterne and the birth of the English novel
1759

C LERIC, wit and inventor of the modern novel, Laurence Sterne is a credit to Yorkshire. Strictly speaking, however, he is not a Yorkshireman. Sterne was born in November 1713 at Clonmel in Ireland. His father Roger, an officer in the British Army was stationed there.

There is no doubting Laurence's Yorkshire pedigree, however. His great-grandfather, Richard Sterne, was Archbishop of York in the reign of James II; his uncle Dr Jacques Sterne was Archdeacon of York.

Laurence had an unsettled childhood, spending his first years in different barracks before being sent to public school at Halifax.

His schooling came to an abrupt end after seven years in 1731 when his father was killed in a duel. He left his son without a penny.

The extended family stepped in to help. First cousin Richard funded Laurence through Jesus College, Cambridge. Soon after his graduation, he was ordained and his uncle the Archdeacon secured him his first living of Sutton-on-the-Forest and a prebend at York.

Unfortunately, uncle and nephew fell out. The official reason was politics: Jacques, an enthusiastic Whig, wanted Laurence to write party propaganda, and he refused. The unofficial reason, as local gossip had it, was sex: both clerics lusted after the same woman. Whatever the cause, the souring of family relations left Sterne with little prospect of preferment.

On Easter Monday 1741 he married rector's daughter Elizabeth Lumley in York Minster. Described as "unattractive and acid tongued" by one writer, she suffered from what would now be termed depression. But she gave him a daughter, Lydia, and a living, Stillington, which was in the gift of her family.

It was not a good living, and Sterne turned to fiction writing to take his mind off his cares. His two-volume novel, The Life and Opinions of Tristram Shandy, Gentlemen, was printed in York, and initially sold in December 1759 by John Hinxman, at the Sign of the Bible, Stonegate, York, and by a London bookseller James Dodsley. It is reckoned to the first true English novel and earned Sterne lasting fame.

Some in York were upset by the book, believing they or their friends had been caricatured by Sterne in Tristram Shandy. Many expressed sympathy for a local doctor, thought to have been distorted into the grotesque character Dr Slop.

But in London, it was an instant hit. Short on plot but full of wit, both literary and bawdy, the book was praised to the skies by London society.

Soon Sterne was the man of the moment. The Bishop of Gloucester gave him a purse filled with guineas, he was a sought-after dinner guest and he had his portrait painted.

Delighted by his success and celebrity, Sterne returned to his Yorkshire parishes, now augmented by Coxwold. He move into the Coxwold parsonage after his house in Stillington burnt down. The new home was rechristened Shandy Hall.

There he led an enjoyable life, writing and shooting in the day, playing his fiddle and flirting with the women in the evening.

He died just before Christmas 1761, on a visit to London.

Millennium Press

Local clergyman is a literary hit!

Sterne's 'novel' takes London critics by storm

COXWOLD clergyman Laurence Sterne has caused a literary storm with his book, The Life and Opinions of Tristram Shandy, Gentleman, which was published in York.

The book, which is written in a new literary form, the 'novel', has been on sale in York for some time but since its release in London, where it is being sold by Mr James Dodsley, a London bookseller, it has been snapped up by the critics and London society.

The novel is described as being short on plot but full of wit and a trifle bawdy, and selling like the proverbial hot cakes.

It is a welcome change of fortune for Mr Sterne, who had the misfortune to be left penniless when his Army officer father was killed in a duel, and later his career in the church seemed at an end but his decision to take up writing for a living has paid handsome dividends.

Laurence Sterne's house at Coxwold, where he wrote his famous 'novel' and which he has renamed 'Shandy Hall' in honour of the hero of his best-selling book

Millennium Press

First patients admitted to Bootham Park Hospital
November 1, 1777

B OOTHAM Park Hospital developed out of the need "to discourage the lower kind of private mad houses". This was one reason given as to why York should possess such an institution at a meeting chaired by the Archbishop of York at York Castle in 1772. The meeting resolved that a lunatic asylum should be built in the city.

This decision was more radical than it sounds today. When the York Lunatic Asylum was opened in 1777 it was only the fifth public asylum to be founded in England.

Mental illness was far from being understood. If a sufferer was poor he was likely to be ignored or oppressed; if he was rich, he would be a target of those "private mad houses" who traded in lunacy.

The most infamous asylum, Bedlam, in London, still exhibited lunatics to the public every Sunday, for the price of a penny. It attracted 100,000 visitors a year. Even royalty was not safe: King George III was deemed mad during this period and was once knocked unconscious by those seeking to restrain him.

A subscription was opened to raise £5,000 to pay for the York asylum. An article in the press outlined why one was needed: "Something should be done for the relief of those unhappy sufferers who are the objects of terror and compassion to all around them, and whose cases lay a just claim to the benevolence of their fellow-creatures."

Moreover, they had nowhere else to go: the workhouse was unsuitable and the County Hospital did not take those of unsound mind.

Unfortunately, when £5,500 had been collected it was found to be insufficient. A further £2,000 was requested by the organising committee. Critics asked if they were building an asylum for the poor or "erecting a palace for the accommodation of the opulent lunatic".

In December 1773 a parcel of land outside Bootham Bar had been purchased. Former Lord Mayor of York and leading city architect John Carr was commissioned to design the building. Lack of money held up its construction, but it finally welcomed its first ten patients in November 1777, at a charge of eight shillings per week.

The asylum governors drew up a formidable list of regulations. Debarred from entry were those discharged as incurable by other asylums, epileptics, idiots and pregnant women, so their children could not claim poor relief.

Men were issued with a uniform consisting of a coat, waistcoat, shirt and breeches, as well as a night-cap. Women had a gown and petticoat, shoes, stockings and aprons.

In the early years, the enlightened ideas of the founders appear to have been largely forgotten. The governors soon altered the rules to allow "affluent" patients into the asylum.

Care of the patients was also causing concern. A Quaker, Hannah Mills, was admitted in 1790 with melancholy and died 14 days later. Her neglect ultimately led the famous York Quaker family the Tukes to found The Retreat on Heslington Lane.

But under new management, Bootham Park Hospital began to improve. By 1948 and the creation of the National Health Service, it was beginning to enjoy a reputation as a leader in its field. It remains the oldest psychiatric hospital in the country still used for its original purpose.

Millennium Press

New hospital opens in York

The new Bootham Hospital, which is promising a new standard of care for mental patients

A NEW hospital has opened in York which promises to revolutionise the care of patients with mental illnesses.

Bootham Hospital, designed by the famous York architect, John Carr, and built with money raised by public subscription - some £7,500 - has been built in spacious grounds just outside

Revolutionary treatment for mental patients promised

Bootham bar.

The splendid red brick building promises patients the best care in fine surroundings. No longer will the poor unfortunates be exhibited to the public for a penny a time, as is the case in

an infamous London asylum.

The asylum is only the fifth such public asylum to be opened in Britain and demonstrates the desire of the citizens of York to care for the less fortunate in their midst.

Ouse Bridge opens
August 19, 1820

*T*HE man who built Ouse Bridge, a landmark in the very heart of York, was (whisper it) a Lancastrian. Only just, mind: Hiram Craven was born just the wrong side of the border in Colne, near Burnley, in 1780.

He crossed into Yorkshire as a young man when he was apprenticed to a stonemason in Oakworth, near Haworth. Later he set up his own business, and it was then that he heard about a project to build a new bridge across the River Ouse in York.

There had most probably first been a bridge near this point in Roman times. In the 12th century, a wooden structure spanned the river here. It collapsed under the weight of the multitude who came to greet the newly appointed Archbishop of York, William Fitz-Herbert, in 1154.

As the crowd fell into the river, the Archbishop made the sign of the cross – so the story goes – and summoned up divine intervention. Certainly no lives were lost, and a chapel was erected on the rebuilt bridge as a token of thanksgiving for the miracle.

It was heavy snow and a severe frost that did for this Ouse Bridge. Two centre arches on the 300-year-old structure buckled in 1564. Twelve houses were destroyed and the same number of people drowned.

The next version lasted into the 19th century, when the council decided that it needed widening. But a survey showed that it would have to be entirely replaced.

After a number of engineers had attempted and failed to construct suitably firm foundations in the fast-flowing river, Hiram Craven arrived in York and agreed to take on the project.

In December 1810, a procession, led by the band of the 4th Dragoon Guards, marched to the site and the Lord Mayor George Peacock laid a foundation stone.

Craven then set to work. He ingeniously sank a number of bales of wool into the river to slow the flow where necessary in order to create the foundations.

Slowly, the bridge began to rise up. It was designed with three arches, the central one boasting a span of 75 feet.

Many of the workmen employed by Craven lived in Hainworth, near Keighley. Incredibly, when work finished on the Saturday they walked 40 miles home, undertaking the return journey on the Monday morning.

It took ten years to complete Ouse Bridge. The first section, 27 feet wide, was opened in January 1818 by a procession of six Royal Mail coaches, the civic party, the York magistrates and many citizens.

Two and a half years later, the entire structure was officially opened. The Lord Mayor presiding over the ceremony was George Peacock, the same man who had laid the foundation stone ten years earlier. He was serving his second term in office in 1820.

For Hiram Craven, personal sadness followed professional triumph. His son Abraham was a victim of the York cholera epidemic in 1832.

But Craven's Ouse Bridge still stands today, carrying more traffic than was ever dreamed of when it was built 180 years ago.

Millennium Press

York gets a new Ouse Bridge

Ten years' work ends as stone masterpiece is opened

YORK has a splendid new Ouse Bridge, which opened today after ten years' hard work by master stone-mason Mr Hiram Craven and his team.

Despite many technical difficulties, not least of which were the problems of building in fast-flowing water, the new three-arch bridge opened on time - although part of the bridge has been open to traffic for the past two years.

The opening ceremony was carried out by the the Lord Mayor, George Peacock, who incidently, laid the foundation stone in 1810 in his first term in office as York's first citizen.

This splendid new Ouse Bridge (above), which replaces the old bridge (right), has now opened

Gas street lighting comes to York

March 22, 1824

A SCOTSMAN living in Cornwall is credited with first using gas commercially. He lit his home in Redruth with coal gas in 1792, and installed gas lighting at a Birmingham factory six years later.

In 1807, the first experiment in street lighting by gas took place in London's Pall Mall. Seventeen years later, York too saw the light.

The public was informed in September, 1822, of the intention of a new firm, the York Gas Light Company, to apply for parliamentary powers. Royal Assent was granted in May the following year.

Among the company's directors were the sitting Lord Mayor, Thomas Smith, and a previous mayor, the chairman George Peacock.

Events moved astonishingly quickly. In July 1823 the company bought two acres of ground near Monk Bridge; by August John Outhett had been appointed to build the works to his design; and on March 22, 1824 the manufacturing and distributing plants were in operation, and gas was being supplied.

"York Lighted By Gas" announced the York Courant the following day. "The Works of the York Gas Light Company having been completed, the principal streets and shops of this City were lighted with gas last evening, and presented a very brilliant appearance.

"The large lamp in the Pavement had a very good effect, and the contrast in all parts was strikingly apparent between the dull and murky glare of the oil lamps with which the City has hitherto been lighted and the brilliant illumination emitted from the gas.

"The fitting up of the lights in several shops, etc., is very splendid, and the large circular light over the door of Mr Barber, at the Black Swan, was generally admired.

"A merry peal from the Cathedral Bells ushered in the introduction of the new era of light in old Ebor, and the streets were thronged with spectators till a late hour."

Take up of the new service was initially slow, because gas was expensive compared to oil. The company began with about 250 private consumers.

There was much public debate as to whether the price for street lighting was too much for the city to bear. But street lighting by gas became general throughout the city from October, 1824.

Because of the unrest over prices, a second company was formed in January 1837, the York Union Gas Light Company, with its works in Hungate. The competition did bring the price of gas down. But it also led to frequent disputes. Gas mains were duplicated, causing unnecessary disruption on the roads.

Consequently, it was considered that the competition was detrimental to customers and the two amalgamated into the York Gas Company. Over the coming years it was to introduce many innovations to the city, including gas meters, gas cookers and gas heating.

In the same year as the first York gasworks was being built, 1823, another influential group was formed. The aim of the Yorkshire Philosophical Society, its first annual report said, was to "promote the interests of science".

Millennium Press

New light shines on city streets

Citizens hail gas lighting

YORK streets will be safer at night from now on thanks to a wonderful modern invention.

Gas lighting, which is supplied by the newly-formed York Gas Light Company, has been used for the first time today to light up some of the city's main thoroughfares, shops and public buildings.

And the scheme has been hailed as a great success, although there have been some complaints about the cost, which is considerably higher than equivalent oil lamps.

But generally the response has been favourable, with the large lamp in Pavement drawing particular comment for its brilliance.

A peal of Minster bells was rung to welcome in the new era and York citizens thronged the street until late to admire the new lighting.

At present the company is only supplying gas for lighting but it is hoped in future to use gas for both cooking and heating.

One of the new-fangled gas lamps used to illuminate the city's Minster

Victoria Cross awarded to York's Crimean War hero
June 26, 1857

ONE of York's bravest sons was buried with full military honours in York Cemetery in 1887. Some 30 years earlier, Thomas Wilkinson became one of the first men in Britain – and certainly the first man in York – to be awarded the Victoria Cross.

Wilkinson was born in Marygate in 1831. He joined the Royal Marines on November 23, 1850, when he was 19.

He was awarded the VC, the country's most prized bravery award, for his heroics during the Crimean War in 1855. Serving with the Royal Marine Artillery of HMS Britannia at Sebastopol he risked his life over a long period of time as he carried sandbags in exposed areas to rebuild gun emplacements.

The medal was presented to him by Queen Victoria in June 1857. It now resides in the Royal Marines' Museum in Portsmouth.

A dedication in Britain's Sea Soldiers says: "With a cool head and dauntless courage this brave member of the Royal Marine Artillery sprang into the very jaws of danger.

"With Russian bullets whizzing round him, with cannons belching forth the fearful volleys, with shells whizzing overhead, he began to repair battery after battery so that our guns had something like good cover from which to reply to the garrison of Sebastopol.

"It is quite impossible to say how many lives were saved by his gallant deed."

Wilkinson left the service when he was 28, married and settled back in York. He died on September 22, 1887, after a long illness, aged 55.

Unfortunately he soon became a forgotten hero. Apart from his military burial, the city did not officially commemorate the courage of this soldier.

Some Russian guns captured at Sebastopol were presented to York in a national share-out after the war ended. It is thought that the city may have been chosen to receive them in recognition of Wilkinson's Victoria Cross.

Originally it was planned to site the guns on St George's Field. Eventually they were placed in buttresses at Blue Bridge, with a plaque in memory of the men who fell during the war.

What subsequently happened to the guns is a mystery. One theory is that they were melted down during the Second World War.

Bombardier Wilkinson's grave was rediscovered, neglected and overgrown, in the 1980s. When members of the Royal Marines Association were informed, they soon set to work. As well as cleaning up the grave, they organised a rededication ceremony in the Cemetery.

Ex-servicemen, officers and reserves gathered to hear the Last Post played over Wilkinson's grave again in 1992 when the association presented an oak seat to York Cemetery Trust to recognise his valour.

Wilkinson is not York's only recipient of the Victoria Cross. Sergeant Harry Blanchard Wood was awarded the same honour for a single-handed action against the Germans in France, while serving with the 2nd Battalion Scots Guards in the First World War.

Millennium Press

Victoria Cross awarded to York marine

York's VC hero, Thomas Wilkinson

YORK man Thomas Wilkinson has been awarded the nation's highest military honour for bravery.

The Marygate-born Royal Marine was presented with the award by Her Majesty, Queen Victoria, in a special ceremony today to mark his actions under fire at the siege of Sebastopol.

Wilkinson was a member of the Royal Marine Artillery crew of HMS Britannia at Sebastopol two years ago during the Crimean War. Despite heavy shellfire from the Russian guns, Wilkinson several times risked his life to repair the defences around his battery.

His actions "in the very jaws of danger" enabled the battery to keep on firing and undoubtedly saved the lives of many of his comrades.

Rowntree family moves into cocoa production
1862

THE long history of Rowntree's, the world famous confectioner, can be traced back to one remarkable woman – Mary Tuke. She came from a prominent Society of Friends family. Her grandfather was one of the 4,000 people imprisoned for their Quaker beliefs in the 1660s. He was jailed at Ouse Bridge.

Mary's father William Tuke was a blacksmith and Freeman of York, who died in 1704.

At the age of 30, Mary took the unusual decision for a woman of the time to set up her own grocery shop. She took on nephew William as an apprentice in 1746, and he inherited the business when she died six years later.

Under his stewardship the shop began to specialise in tea and coffee, and by 1763 was selling Churchman's Patent Chocolate from Bristol.

William's son Henry had followed him into the business, and they began the manufacture of cocoa and chocolate around 1785. But it wasn't until the mid-19th century that the business was acquired by the Rowntree family.

They originally came from Hutton Rudby in Cleveland. In the late 1600s, one of the family was cast out because he joined the Society of Friends.

He moved to Pickering and his son, John Rowntree, began a grocery business in Scarborough. In turn his son Joseph founded a similar business at 28 Pavement, York.

Later he was commissioned to investigate the effects of famine in Ireland. On that trip he took his 12-year-old son, also called Joseph.

Joseph junior was destined to transform York's industrial history and turn the Rowntree name into a household word. That Irish trip was to have a profound impact on him, shaping his paternalistic attitude to his workforce in later years.

After his father's death, Joseph became a partner with his older brother in the family shop at Pavement. Younger brother Henry Isaac Rowntree purchased the Tuke's cocoa and chocolate business in Coppergate in 1862.

Two years later he transferred it to Tanner's Moat. But Henry was not a successful businessman. Much of his time was given to Quaker and temperance affairs and he didn't understand the technical side of trading.

In 1869, Joseph left the grocery business and joined Henry at the cocoa works. At this time its major product was Prize Medal Rock Cocoa. This was prepared from fine cocoa mixed with sugar and sold in irregular cakes.

Rowntree's also sold homeopathic cocoa and cocoa powder, made by mixing the ground cocoa with different proportions of sugar and some form of starch, such as sago flour or arrowroot.

Joseph saw that demand was changing. Consumers preferred the purer cocoa essence, and after spending much time and money he managed to perfect the method and produced Rowntree's Elect Cocoa.

Sales increased and the business expanded. In 1890 it was decided to move from Tanner's Moat. A 24-acre site was purchased and building began at a site off Haxby Road.

The development of the railways gave Joseph Rowntree the chance to sell his confectionery further afield. Trade was really taking off.

Millennium Press

Rowntree branches out into cocoa trade

York grocer buys out Tuke's Coppergate business

HENRY Isaac Rowntree, partner in the famous family grocery store in Pavement, York, has bought out the Tuke family's long-established cocoa and chocolate works in Coppergate.

This change in directions by the Rowntree family is seen as a significant move by the Quakers, who have been heavily involved in York business since the family moved to York from Scarborough.

Joseph Rowntree senior, famous for his investigation into famine in

Chocolate making at Joseph Rowntree's newly-purchased cocoa and chocolate works

Ireland, established the Pavement grocery store as one of York's finest, and his sons, Joseph jnr and Henry, have carried on the family tradition.

Now they have decided to go into manufacturing industry as well and if Henry can make a go of the cocoa works, it is believed that York itself could benefit in the form of increased employment.

The founding of York Rugby Club
1868

FOOTBALL may be the beautiful game and an English pastime for the best part of a millennium, but it was rugby that was the rage in the 19th century. The birth of the game is lost in history and shrouded in legend but what is certain is that it was seen as a potent arm of that Victorian moral movement, 'Muscular Christianity', which aimed at producing Christian young men healthy in body and mind. Rugby fitted the bill admirably.

Legend has it that the game started at Rugby School - hence the name - when William Webb Ellis simply picked up the ball during a game of football and ran with it. The tale is almost certainly apocryphal but rugby was certainly developed and nurtured at the public schools and universities and the first recorded game of what was then just rugby (the split between League and Union wouldn't come until 1895) took place at Cambridge in 1839. It's not certain when rugby was first played in York but it was almost certainly by the boys of St Peter's School, who nurtured the infant game, despite an almost total lack of interest from the newspapers of the day. The game was different from today: emphasis was still on kicking the ball and the scoring system reflected that; hacking (another name for tripping) was legal and loose mauls often involved most of the players and went on endlessly.

Sooner or later a senior club would have to be formed in the city. After all, all those pupils weaned on the game at school, needed somewhere to play after they left. The driving force behind the senior club is believed to be a former St Peterite, Robert H Christison, son of the passenger manager of the North Eastern Railway Company in York, and said to be one of the finest centres of his day. No high-powered meeting like that at Huddersfield's George Hotel, which saw the breakaway of the Rugby League clubs, for Christison. Instead he fixed up the sandwiches first!

Christison called on a Mrs Scott, who lived in a house facing Knavesmire, and asked if she would be willing to provide the refreshments for a group of chaps wanting to play a few games of rugby. When she agreed, Christison summoned a meeting of interested parties in her parlour and York Amateur Rugby Club was born.

No record exists of where the club's first match in 1868 was played or who the opponents were. All that is known is that York lost, for it was to be three seasons before they won a game - and that was a soccer match against York Training College.

As to the venue, it might well have been near Terry's factory at Bustardthorpe for early matches were played 'on the banks of the Ouse' before flooding drove them to seek a new pitch. Several early games were played on Knavesmire. At this time the club's only assets were a pair of portable goalposts!

Finally a permanent pitch - the one used for many years by Southlands ARL - was secured on Knavesmire before moves to the Yorkshire Gentlemen's Cricket Ground (now buried under York District Hospital) and Poad's Field off Fulford Road.

Finally they first rented and later bought Clarence Street, their home for 104 years until their move to their current home at Monks Cross in 1989. At Clarence Street they joined the Northern Union and when the big split came in 1895, York stayed loyal to the Union code - for two years, before opting for Rugby League.

York has had its ups and downs over the years but it has remained a professional club since that 1897 switch, and have enjoyed some success, appearing at Wembley (as losing finalists) in 1931, and winning the second division championship in 1981 as well as a handful of Yorkshire Cup victories - all a far cry from those portable goalposts and Mrs Scott's sandwiches!

Millennium Press

York gets new sporting club

First 'rugby' team is founded in the city

THE new sport of Rugby has gained a foothold in the city with the founding of York Amateur Rugby Club.

The driving force behind the club is Mr Robert H Christison, an old boy of St Peter's School, York, and son of the passenger manager for the North Eastern Railway Company in York.

The new 15-a-side game of Rugby Football is thought to derive from soccer, although the players are allowed to handle the ball and tackles can be made with both arms and legs. It was developed in the public schools of southern England and a match has been recorded at

Players train for the new sport of Rugby which has gained a foothold in York

Cambridge as early as 1839.

Legend has it that one William Webb Ellis, a pupil at Rugby School (hence the name) started the game by picking up the ball and running with it during a game of soccer, but this cannot be verified.

The game took a hold at St Peter's School and it is believed that many of the current team are Peterites.

The new club hopes to play matches in the Knavesmire area, where Mrs Scott has agreed to provide after-match teas for the players.

York Railway Station opens
June 25, 1877

Y ORK'S new railway station opened to great public acclaim. The first train left for Scarborough on time at 5.30am. Trains then came and went throughout the day.

It was a colourful scene. Crowds milled on the new platforms to see the imposing locomotives. Most of the engines were in the green North Eastern Railway livery. Different shades allowed onlookers to guess which of the company's four locomotive works had carried out the work.

Passengers filled the first and second class NER coaches, in their distinctive dark plum shade, and were packed into the dark green third class carriages.

When York Railway Station opened, it was the largest in Britain. Railway bosses and guests at the grand opening were lost in admiration for the architectural achievement.

They gazed in awe at the 800ft long and 234ft wide train-shed roof. The largest span, over the through tracks, measures 81ft.

The wrought iron roof ribs rise to 42ft above the platforms, and are held in place by cast-iron columns. And the main platform is fully 1,500ft long.

When it was completed, owner North Eastern Railways declined to give an exact cost for the station, but it was thought to be in the region of £400,000.

There was only one dissenting voice at the grand opening. One NER shareholder called it "a very splendid monument of extravagance".

But railway chiefs and the travelling public were delighted with the new building. For 30 years progress in York had been stymied by an inadequate station.

The city can trace its railway heritage back to 1835 when the York & Midland Railway Company was formed, largely under the influence of George Hudson.

The "Railway King", as he was known, realised the potential of this wonderful form of transport and vowed to 'Mek' all t'railways cum t'York!"

By the late 1830s, construction of the York & North Midland line was progressing well. So well, in fact, that a makeshift wooden station had to be constructed.

This served its purpose until 1841 when York's first station-proper was built just inside the city walls. Hudson had persuaded the Great North of England Railway to bring its line from Darlington to York, instead of Leeds, and the station was designed by local architect, George Townsend Andrews.

Traffic at the station increased rapidly, soon placing it under strain. Rail access was restricted by the size of the archway through the city walls.

These difficulties were exacerbated by the fact that the station was a terminus. Trains between north and south had to reverse direction before continuing their journeys, causing delays and congestion.

Permission for the new station was obtained from Parliament in 1866, but it took 11 years before it opened.

The North Eastern Railway's architect, Thomas Prosser, drew up the original plans for the station. He based his design for the train-shed on that produced by John Dobson for Newcastle Central Station, with some features derived from the roof at Paddington, partly designed by Isambard Kingdom Brunel.

Disputes and a strike by workmen held up the construction in the early part of the 1870s. But the end result was a station of which the city could be proud.

Millennium Press

York on fast track to railway success

£400,000 new station is Britain's largest

Y ORK'S splendid new railway station opened today to public acclaim - and just one dissenting voice.

Amidst the celebrations, one shareholder of North Eastern Railways complained that the reputed £400,000 it had cost to build the new station was "a splendid monument of extravagance".

But his was a lone voice as the crowds flocked in to admire the new station and witness the colourful scene as engines and carriages in the different liveries of various rail companies vied with each other to provide the greatest spectacle.

Staff and trains at York's splendid new railway station which opened today

But it was the station itself which drew the greatest gasps. With a main platform more than 1,500 feet long and splendid ribs and columns of the wrought iron roof, this is Britain's largest station - and surely its most impressive?

The new station, built outside the city walls, replaces the old station close-by, which is now too small to cope with the increased traffic.

Trams come to York
October, 1880

TRAMWAY mania struck England in the 1870s. All the major cities were buying into this revolutionary new form of transport. The York Tramway Company was formed in 1880 to build a line for horse drawn trams from Fulford to York. In October of that year the opening ceremony began with a luncheon at Harkers Hotel. The civic party was later conveyed by tram from the Castle Mills Bridge terminus to Fulford. They returned on a steam powered tram.

The tramway was soon extended. It could take passengers from the Barracks to Nessgate to the Mount. In order to pull a tram up Micklegate hill, an extra horse was added to the normal two.

The York Tramway Company did not treat its horses well. Pictures show the beasts looking exhausted, with their ribcages clearly visible.

York's tramway horses apparently worked longer hours, pulled the cars longer distances and were given less food than was the normal practice elsewhere.

Figures for 11 towns and cities running horse-tram systems in 1889-90 show that the 37 horses pulling York cars each covered nearly 18 miles a day, the highest mileage in the table. York also had the lowest annual cost per animal.

Moreover, the horses actually brought in some revenue – via the sale of their manure.

Horse-drawn trams left York's streets on September 7, 1909. A black-edged card was issued to mark their passing. It stated: "In loving remembrance of the York (Horse) Trams. Gone but not forgotten. May they rest in peace."

The electric trams had arrived. Wider tracks had to be removed to make way for a narrower gauge for the electric version.

Queen Street was widened at a cost of £500 in 1907 to take the new transport. Lendal Bridge was strengthened for the same reason.

York's first electric tramcar, decorated with flags and bunting, ran from Fulford to Nessgate in January 1910. After the upheaval of the preparations, it was enthusiastically received by the crowds who lined the streets to watch it.

The first woman tram driver was Alice Heppell. She was taken on, despite union opposition, because of the shortage of men in the First World War. However, the union action was not entirely fruitless – she was the only successful woman applicant from a list of 21.

York Station was the tramway centre. Extra track was laid for race meetings; at the end of each day, trams queued from the Knavesmire Hotel to the top of Balmoral Terrace to take racegoers home.

Trams were not always the most comfortable way to travel. In winter, if you failed to squeeze in on the lower deck, it meant being exposed to the elements in the open top.

Seats were built from narrow slats. The seat backs could be moved to and fro so passengers could always face the way they were travelling.

The drivers operated the tram from open compartments at either end. Conductors would punch and distribute the tickets, which were coloured differently for the different stages.

After the Great War, all tramways began losing money. Electric trams lasted until 1935 in York until buses took over completely.

Millennium Press

October 1880   **A thousand years of York's history**

New transport system unveiled

One of the new horse-drawn trams at Fulford

YORK'S newest transport systems rolled into action today with the official opening of the York-Fulford tramway service.

After an opening ceremony and luncheon at Harker's Hotel, the civic party was conveyed from the terminus at Castle

New service will link city centre to Fulford village

Mills Bridge to Main Street, Fulford by horse-drawn tram. The party later returned by a steam-driven tram.

If the new service is a success, it is hoped to

extend it through the city to the Mount, although it is envisaged that the passage up Micklegate hill will require an extra horse to the normal two used to pull the trams.

The first edition of the Evening Press
October 2, 1882

WILLIAM Wallace Hargrove was very much a man of the 80s - the 1880s that is - although the go-ahead Conservative businessman would have been just as well at home in the 1980s of Mrs Thatcher's Britain.

The Hargrove family was steeped in newspapers but whereas his father, William senior, was a man of letters who turned to newspaper publishing, young William was a thrusting entrepreneur with a nose for a good deal and not averse to using his newspapers to put across his political views.

Hargrove snr had got into printing back in 1813 when he and son John purchased the Yorkshire Herald, then printed in a couple of rooms above the counting house in Coney Street.

By the time William jnr joined the firm as a partner in 1856, William snr had turned the Herald from a quaint county weekly into the leading morning daily of Yorkshire and Durham, and the Coney Street office into a printing centre with the most modern equipment. He was also instrumental in lobbying the Government to cut stamp duty on newspapers, and he set up a wide-ranging team of local correspondents - a move which still serves the Evening Press well.

But William snr was a conservative with both a small and a large 'C' and William jnr was champing at the bit. His chance came when William snr retired to the Isle of Wight, leaving William a prosperous company and a flagship newspaper, the Yorkshire Herald, which he had turned from a 7d, four-page weekly into a 1d, eight-page daily.

But William wanted more. The rise of literacy amongst the Victorian working class was a resource waiting to be tapped - and Hargrove was the man to tap it.

The result was the Evening Press (it didn't become the 'Yorkshire Evening Press' until early the next century, before reverting to its original title in 1996), launched on Monday, October 2, 1882.

It sold for just ½d and its mixture of court cases, county gossip, sport and local business news was an instant hit. His string of local correspondents kept the paper ahead of its rivals in news coverage and his up-to-date printing equipment gave him a significant advantage.

The paper had mass appeal and whereas the Herald was very much a country paper, the Press appealed to town and country alike. Its audience was mainly in the towns, especially York, but Hargrove's clever use of the railways meant an efficient distribution system which made the paper readily available throughout the county.

Indeed the conservative Hargrove used the railways to put one over on his great rivals, the liberal Rowntree family on more than one occasion. The Rowntrees' political stronghold was Darlington and by using the railways, Hargrove was able to send copies of the Evening Press into the heart of his enemies' territory, often containing disparaging articles about the great chocolate family.

But it will be as a newspaper innovator that Hargrove will be remembered. His 'baby' is still going strong 117 years later and the principles he established for producing a popular and successful newspaper still apply.

Millennium Press

York gets a new evening paper

Hargrove promises a paper for the people

YORK has a new evening paper, the Evening Press, and proprietor William Wallace Hargrove has promised that the new evening paper will be a paper for the ordinary working man.

Hargrove has an impressive newspaper pedigree. His father, William senior, and elder brother John, purchased the Yorkshire Herald in 1813 and turned the flagging, 7d, four-page weekly into a thriving 1d, eight-page daily.

The Hargrove firm, which William junior joined in 1856, has also turned the Herald's base in Coney Street, York, into one of the most efficient

William Wallace Hargrove, proprietor of York's new evening daily paper, The Evening Press

and modern printing operations in the country.

Using that technology - and the extensive railway network in the county - Hargrove junior intends to make his new paper,

which costs just ½d, and is packed with court reports, gossip, business news and sport, as well as news from local correspondents, the best in the country.

Queen Victoria's Diamond Jubilee

June 22, 1897

*I*T was the biggest celebration of the year. Every day for the first six months of 1897, the Evening Press had printed the latest details about the preparation for the diamond jubilee of Queen Victoria's accession to the throne.

The day itself began with a peal of the Minster bells at 8.30am. Dull and overcast weather soon gave way to sunshine.

Business had been almost entirely suspended for the day and colourful bunting decorated every street. The Evening Press correspondent was impressed: "A general view of the city at once revealed that a holiday was being kept for, from almost every tower – and York boasts many towers – there floated the Union Jack or some other indication of the loyalty of the city."

Amongst the features the Press picked out as being especially fine were the Yorkshire Club, Lendal Bridge and Coney Street, the latter boasting Royal Standards and banners as well as the Union Jack.

Clifford's Tower was also flying the flag as was the Assize Courts. Many fluttered high above Stonegate.

Celebrations took different forms in different parts of the city. At the Infantry Barracks, the Army paraded before Colonel Harington, commanding officer of the 14th Regimental District.

At the day's heart were the school children. Nearly 14,000 York children, accompanied by 1,300 teachers, assembled in the Dean's Park, Duncombe Place and Parliament Street before marching to the Bootham Asylum Field. There, they formed a huge crowd around musical director Mr Mills. He ascended the stand to lead them in singing God Save The Queen.

Later the children had tea and took part in various games. More than 1,000 aged poor were also entertained to tea.

Meanwhile, the Lord Mayor, Sheriff and Corporation attended a special service of thanksgiving at the Minster. It was actually a double celebration for the Lord Mayor, Christopher Annakin Milward, who was knighted in the Queen's jubilee honours.

At night, the skies over York were lit up – firstly through fireworks, and then with a searchlight sweeping the city from the central tower of the Minster.

In Malton, there was tree planting, a gala and three separate processions. A cask of beer was donated to the people in the town's workhouse.

Scarborough's main event was the laying of the foundation stone on the new Marine Drive. Shops and businesses were closed in Ripon as it was observed as a holiday.

But the event was not free of dissenting voices. Prompted by the pomp surrounding the jubilee season, some were openly discussing the idea of Britain becoming a republic.

The Evening Press leader took against such radical opinions, stressing the value for money given by the monarchy.

"It is very questionable whether royalty is in itself more costly than republicanism, to say nothing of the indirect benefits arising from it.

"Thus, according to statistics published, the annual amount voted to the Queen is less than the amount derived by Parliament from the Crown lands which were given up in exchange."

Millennium Press

June 22, 1897   A thousand years of York's history

60 glorious years

York helps celebrate Queen's diamond jubilee

Her Majesty, Queen Victoria, who today celebrates 60 years on the throne of Great Britain and Ireland

YORK was today helping celebrate sixty glorious years on the throne of Great Britain and Ireland, of her Majesty, Queen Victoria.

Colourful bunting could be found in abundance throughout the city and the Royal Standard and Union Jacks fluttered from many a flagpole and tower.

All the city's schoolchildren, nearly 14,000 of them, accompanied by 1,300 teachers, marched to Bootham Asylum Field, for singing, games and a splendid tea.

The civic party took part in a special service of thanksgiving at the Minster.

Later tonight fireworks and a special searchlight display are planned to round off the celebrations.

Seebohm Rowntree's pioneering report on York poverty
1899

*M*UCH of York was in poverty at the end of the 19th century. In areas like Walmgate and Hungate, families lived in squalor. One man did more than any other to draw attention to the situation: Benjamin Seebohm Rowntree. One of the great reforming Rowntree dynasty, Seebohm was appalled by the living conditions of the city's poorest people.

He worked as a chemist at the cocoa works. Later he turned his scientific mind to the causes of the social distress of poverty. Seebohm's first survey of the working class population of York, Poverty, A Study of Town Life, was published in 1899 and updated in 1901. With his research team, he began by visiting households which did not employ servants, and counting the people who looked poor. Rowntree's definition of a poor family was one showing "obvious want and squalor". They visited 11,560 families, seeing a total of 46,754 people. Of these he classed more than 20,300 as visibly poor – one quarter of York's population.

Next he set out to find out whether they were deprived because they wasted income, or because their income was insufficient. He devised and costed a diet which could just maintain "merely physical efficiency" in a healthy person. Adding the minimum sums for rent, clothing, heating and other essentials he came up with an income defined as the primary poverty line – a level of income on which no one could actually live. He found that 7,230 depended on incomes at or below this level. The main reasons for this penury included low wages, large families, and the death of the chief wage earner.

Seebohm's survey was revolutionary because he linked slum housing and ill health with poverty. Nearly nine tenths of the city's working class housing was inadequate. But as long as the families were paying nearly a third of their incomes in rent, they could not afford to improve their conditions. His survey also found that poverty stunted growth. The poorest 13-year-old boys were three inches shorter and 11lbs lighter than their peers from the better-off working class.

By 1908, York Corporation had begun to take action to improve the worst areas of the city. In that year, Edmund M Smith, medical officer of health, issued his Report On The Sanitary Conditions Of The Hungate District. Whole streets of back-to-back houses were condemned as unfit for human habitation and ordered to be pulled down. Smith repeated the exercise for Walmgate in 1914. Here is an extract of what he found:

"The district is honeycombed with courts and alleys... They mostly contain a few back-to-back or not-through houses, many of them damp, dilapidated or requiring considerable repair and improvement, or without free access of light and air, some of them with foul privy-middens or other obsolete closet accommodation...

"Back yards. The back yards in Hope Street and Albert Street and in some other quarters can only be viewed with repulsion – they are so small and fetid, and so hemmed-in by surrounding houses and other buildings... There are no amenities; it is an absolute slum."

Smith's recommendations were simple: pull down much of the housing and improve that which could be saved.

Millennium Press

York poverty: a city's shame

Rowntree report reveals sad state of city's poor

A DAMNING report by social reformer Seebohm Rowntree has branded the city of York as one of the most squalid in Europe.

Poor housing, low wages and large families contribute to dreadful conditions and a standard of living so low for many of the citizens, that a mere basic existence is all they can hope for.

Rowntree, a member of the famous chocolate family, employed a team of researchers to visit more than 11,000 homes in the city.

They discovered:

● 20,300 in the city are 'visibly poor'

● 7,230 citizens live on or below the basic subsistence level

● poor housing leads to ill-health: 13-year-old boys from poor families are on average three inches shorter and 11lbs lighter than boys from better-off homes.

Rowntree is now working on an updated version of his report which he hopes to publish in 1901. In the meantime, pressure is being put on the city council to do something to ease the suffering of York's poorest inhabitants.

Hungate: one the areas slammed as unfit for human habitation by Seebohm Rowntree's report

The First Aeroplane lands in York
February 21, 1913

O RVILLE and Wilbur Wright undertook the first manned, powered flight in 1903. The honour of being the first aviator to land in York went to Captain Longcroft, of the Royal Flying Corps ten years later.

The date was February 21, 1913, and thousands flocked to Knavesmire to witness his arrival. At this time planes were not only a novelty, but unreliable enough to turn pilots into death-defying heroes.

Captain Longcroft flew one of five aircraft which had taken off from Farnborough in Hampshire on route for their new base in Scotland. Around 7,000 people watched him depart in his fragile biplane for Newcastle.

Two years earlier, the people of Harrogate had witnessed powered flight for the first time. The Daily Mail had organised a Circuit of Britain Air Race in 1911, offering £10,000 to the winner – the world's largest prize.

First stop was at Harrogate. The Yorkshire spa town turned out to be a hugely popular spectator point. A huge wooden grandstand had been erected on the stray. Its 450 yards of seating was packed with 50,000 people paying between sixpence and five shillings to see the men in their flying machines. On top of the stand were three acetylene lamps in case of night flying.

One of the main attractions was flight pioneer Samuel Franklin Cody, an ex-Texan cowboy.

Cody came in from the wrong direction, and just missed the roof of the Royal Hotel. The crowds greeted the first Englishman to reach Harrogate, James Valentine, with a rendering of 'All My Life, I'll Be Your Valentine', before he moved on to Newcastle.

In May 1914, a North Yorkshire flying trip ended in tragedy. A plane with the No 2 Squadron Flying Corps was using the Knavesmire as a staging point on a journey from Montrose to Netheravon.

The eternal enemy of aviation, a thick fog, descended on the North Riding. In the gloom, the crew crashed at Hutton Bonville, Northallerton on its way to York.

Despite the interest in flight, York had to wait an entire generation before boasting its own aerodrome. On Saturday July 4, 1936, the York City Municipal Aerodrome at Clifton was officially opened by Viscount Swinton, Secretary of State for Air.

In his speech, he said: "When you are responsible for the conduct of a great city, you have to take a comprehensive view of your duties, responsibilities and opportunities.

"You are adding a material asset to your city by making this aerodrome."

In June 1937, the aerodrome hosted its first Air Pageant. It was a huge success, attracting a crowd of 10,000 people to watch a three lap air race. The winner clocked up speeds of 117.5 mph.

Among the competitors that day was a German contingent. Only two years later, England and German pilots faced each other in a much more deadly contest.

When war broke out, all civil flying ceased. York Aerodrome was requisitioned by the military. From 1941 it was the site of a huge operation to repair damaged Halifax bombers.

Millennium Press

Air power

Air power came to York today when the first ever landing of an aeroplane in the city occurred on Knavesmire

Historic flight touches down on Knavesmire

HISTORY was made in York today when an aeroplane landed on Knavesmire - the first such occurrence by one of the new flying machines.

Captain Longcroft, of the Royal Flying Corps, was one of five RFC pilots flying from Farnborough in Hampshire to their new base in Scotland.

Around 7,000 people watched the fragile machine land on the grass before taking off again on the next leg of his flight to Newcastle.

The first heavier-than-air machine, built and flown by the Wright brothers, Orville and Wilbur, flew just ten years ago in Kitty Hawk, USA.

Britain, which can claim the first flying pioneer in Yorkshire inventor Sir George Cayley, soon followed suit and just two years ago the Daily Mail newspaper offered the fabulous sum of £10,000 for the winner of their Circuit of Britain Air Race.

Thousands flocked to Harrogate to watch the race, 50,000 people paying to watch the flying machines - not without danger. Samuel Cody, the daring American pilot, flew in from the wrong direction and almost clipped the top of the Royal Hotel.

Thankfully there were no such problems on Knavesmire.

The First World War breaks out

August 4, 1914

W AR erupted in Europe after Archduke Francis Ferdinand, heir to the Hapsburg thrones, was assassinated at Sarajevo on June 28 1914. A month later, Austria-Hungary declared war on Serbia and by August 1, Germany had declared war against Russia. Britain and France, after issuing an ultimatum to the Kaiser, went to war on August 4. Britain's declaration of war on Germany came on August 4. The mobilisation of the reserve forces had an instant effect on York.

At home, people were preparing themselves for Britain's involvement. In York, there was evidence of panic buying. The experience of Mr Banks, of Messrs Banks & Co, the provisions dealers in Nessgate, was typical: "This morning we had dozens of sides of bacon and hundreds of hams," he told the Yorkshire Evening Press on August 1, "but now at three o'clock we have cleared out every ounce of bacon.

"We have sold this morning well over 400 hams, whereas our usual morning sale is rarely more than 30 or 40.

"In regard to foodstuffs, such as butter and lard and all kinds of tinned fruits, we have had an enormous turn and have sold out of many kinds."

The city was filled with soldiers, standing at street corners, travelling to and from barracks in cars and on motor cycles. Hundreds of Army reservists were waiting to join their regiments. Several York post offices stayed open all night to pay them transport money.

The state of alert led to a case of war jitters at Scarborough. A group of voluntary workers stationed at the town's Territorial camp were returning there when guards armed with bayoneted guns told them: "Hands up or we fire!"

This war would be very different to the recent conflicts in South Africa and the Balkans, as a leader in the Evening Press leader column of August 6 acknowledged. It was "destined to put to the immediate test a vast range and variety of ideas and inventions, elements and experiments, and to assume a dimension and a character fundamentally and wholly different from anything hitherto known to the science of naval and military warfare".

Technology had given the forces the seaplane, torpedo and submarine, the aeroplane and the airship, and wireless telegraphy.

By mid August, York was adjusting to the new circumstances. Schools, including Fishergate and Park Grove, had been commandeered by the military and strenuous efforts were being made to find temporary accommodation for the displaced children.

Seventy Boy Scouts who had been serving as messengers for the military authorities at York for about a year made an appeal for more bicycles to carry out their increased duties.

And the public was disbarred from the City Baths at St George's Fields after 3.30pm so the troops could use them.

A "Call to Arms" was published in the Press. Lord Kitchener wanted another 100,000 men, aged between 19 and 30, to join the army. "Terms of service: general service for a period of three years or until the war is concluded."

The response was tremendous, as the newspaper reported. "Scenes of the greatest enthusiasm have been enacted every hour and recruits, instead of coming in tens and twenties, have come by the hundred."

Millennium Press

August 4, 1914   **A thousand years of York's history**

Britain at war!

Pickering Territorials march off to war

WAR preparations got under way today after Germany ignored Britain and France's ultimatum to withdraw from Russia.

The events which started in Sarajevo on June 28, 1914, with the assasination of Archduke Francis Ferdinand, heir to the Hapsburgs, spiralled to their inevitable conclusion today with the Allies'

Panic buying as Allies declare war on Germany

declaration of war on Germany, an event which is likely to plunge the whole world into war.

Meanwhile at home, men are flocking to the call to arms, with a steady flood of volunteers and lots of regular soldiers in

the city.

However, there have been signs of panic buying with one city centre provisions merchant reporting a run on sides of bacon and hams. The store sold out its entire stock within a day.

The Armistice: First World War ends

November 11, 1918

*T*HE excitement and enthusiasm that followed the outbreak of war seemed like a million years ago. After a conflict that had decimated a generation of young men, and imposed hardships on the British people not previously experienced, it was an exhausted but joyful nation that embraced peace.

The German delegates signed the terms of capitulation at 5am in the morning. At 11am, fighting stopped on all fronts.

"The anxieties of Armageddon are ended," stated the Yorkshire Evening Press in its first peacetime edition in four years. "The last sacrifice has been made at the altar of Mars. The world has been saved for freedom and fair-play. Through the terror we have reached the triumph."

The Lord Mayor announced the Armistice on the steps of the Mansion House. People took to the streets in rapture. In scenes replicated all over the country, the citizens of York came together to rejoice.

The Minster bells gave forth a joyous peal of peace. Crowds surrounded the paper sellers to read the news they had waited so long for.

Tears of sorrow, joy and pride were openly wept. Soon flags were appearing across the city. People decked themselves in patriotic colours. At the Lord Mayor's request businesses closed and gave employees the rest of the day off.

A service of thanksgiving was held at the Minster at 12.30pm. Fully 10,000 people assembled there. The nave and the transepts were filled and the vast congregation spilled out into the choir aisle.

The hymn All People That On Earth Do Dwell was sung before the Dean led the service in prayers.

He then addressed the congregation: "This is no opportunity for a sermon, as I am quite sure you will all agree. At the same time it is an occasion for recollection.

"The war is over. Hostilities ceased, we are informed, at 11 o'clock this morning. The guns that have roared and thundered for 4½ long years are silent; the murderous business is done. Thank God!"

He concluded by looking ahead: "And let us gird up our loins here before God for the work that lies before us; filled with the strong love of God, there is no other inspiration.

"Under the Father's guidance, we will work as we have never worked before for the brotherhood of man."

At the police court, chairman of the bench Mr JJ Hunt stopped proceedings at 11am. "It is a happy day for our nation, and for the many nations that have been engaged in this dreadful war," he said.

"I hope it might be the beginning of a real peace, and that we may soon be able to welcome back home those who had done such good service to the country."

York's Liberal MP Arnold Rowntree spoke of how he had considered resigning his position at the start of the war because his religious conviction prevented him taking arms. But he was persuaded to change his mind.

He said: "We are all feeling that a new era begins today. After four years of agonising ordeal we greet the new dawn with feelings of thankfulness...

"There is a burning desire in us all that in these fateful days we might be worthy of the trust that has been placed upon us."

Millennium Press

Armistice!

The flags and bunting are put up as residents ofMillfield Road, York, celebrate the end of the war

THE war to end all wars came to an end today as the Allies and Germany signed an Armistice agreement that put an immediate end to the fighting.

The German delegates signed the terms of capitulation today, with the Armistice coming into effect at 11 minutes past 11 on November 11.

The news of the

York celebrates as terrible slaughter comes to an end

Armistice was announced by the Lord Mayor from the steps of York Mansion House.

People took to the streets in scenes of rapture and many a tear was spilt.

The Minster bells sound-ed a special peal and 10,000 people assembled there soon after midday for a special service of thanksgiving.

Businesses closed and many workers got the rest of the day off work as the nation rejoiced.

York's first municipal park opens

July 16, 1921

ROWNTREE Park, York's first municipal park, arose out of the carnage of the First World War. The Rowntrees, a peace-loving Quaker family, had lost many of their factory workers in the battlefields of France and Belgium. They wanted to create a memorial to those who "fell and suffered".

So in 1919 they bought 19 acres of land alongside the River Ouse from the Ecclesiastical Commissioners, the York Corporation bought an additional five acres, and architect Fred Rowntree set about designing a public park for use by all the people of York.

Joseph Rowntree officially handed over the deeds to the then Lord Mayor, Alderman Edward Walker, in a formal ceremony before the public was allowed to try it out.

Rowntree Park opened on July 16, 1921, and it became an immediate hit with the children of that time.

The Yorkshire Evening Press reporter was certainly impressed, particularly with the snack bar "where those who wish may obtain hot water free of charge".

Mischief-makers were kept in check by the first park-keeper James "Parkie" Bell, a well-known and fondly regarded character who policed the park until his death in 1945.

Children thought he had eyes in the back of his head. There was little that got away from Parkie as he surveyed the scene from his hut next to the tennis courts. But the first naughty children knew that they had been rumbled was when they heard the shrill blast of his whistle. The park-keeper would then shake his walking stick and tell them in his distinctive cockney accent to "clear orf".

In those days, the park had several unusual features. These included an aviary full of exotic birds, and a small pond, decorated with a long-gone statue of Eros. No one knows what happened to the statue.

The children's play area boasted wooden swings and a sandy floor to provide a soft landing. There was also a paddling pool.

The sunken rose garden had to be raised after regularly falling victim to floods.

Only the base of the bandstand remains today, but the full structure hosted regular concerts for many years. Military bands would perform and Waddington's music company would play gramophone records every Wednesday.

Waitresses, complete with white aprons and caps, served refreshments from the café.

A tennis tournament was held every summer with the Lord Mayor as guest of honour. Spectators would watch the sport from a specially constructed stand.

In winter, the pond would often freeze over and become a makeshift ice rink. On one occasion, a group of young skaters were posing for a photograph when the ice gave way. There was no danger, however – the water is only a couple of feet deep.

During the war, the Government encouraged a Holidays at Home scheme. Rowntree Park was one of the venues and special events were organised to take people's minds off the hardship. Donkeys were even supplied to give the children rides.

Rowntree Park was not the only one to open in the 1920s. Hull Road Park opened in 1928.

Millennium Press

July 16, 1921   **A thousand years of York's history**

Rowntree Park opens to public

Municipal amenity is a credit to the city

YORK'S first municipal leisure park, Rowntree Park, opened today to great acclaim.

The 24-acre site boasts a variety of amenities to be enjoyed by adults and children alike.

Local youngsters enjoy the amenities at the newly-opened Rowntree Park, York's first municipal park

The landscaped park boasts a cafe, boating lake, sunken gardens, a bandstand, lawns, an aviary, tennis courts, a paddling pool for the younger children and a play area with swings and soft sand base.

In charge of all this, and making sure unruly children don't run wild, is park-keeper James 'Parkie' Bell, who will operate from a hut near the tennis courts.

The park, commissioned by the Rowntree family, and designed by architect Fred Rowntree, is intended as a lasting memorial to the many Rowntree workers who fell on the battlefields of France and Belgium during the Great War.

In 1919 the Rowntree family purchased 19 acres of land alongside Terry Avenue. York Corporation purchased another five acres.

The deeds to the park were handed over by Joseph Rowntree to the Lord Mayor, Alderman Edward Walker in a special ceremony before the public was let in to try the park's amenities.

The Second World War begins
September 3, 1939

*B*RITAIN declared war on Germany on Sunday, September 3, 1939. But preparations for conflict had begun some years before. Hitler's intentions became ever more ominous as his grip on Germany tightened. In 1936, his forces marched into the Rhineland. Two years later his troops crossed the border into Austria. That summer British Prime Minister Neville Chamberlain met with Hitler and returned to declare "peace in our time".

It turned out to be a short peace. But it bought more time for preparations.

In York, the first Air Raid Precautions meeting took place in February, 1937. In the last summer of peace in 1939, glorious sunshine added an air of unreality to the warmongering manoeuvres in Europe.

Blackouts were being practised in York. These rehearsals led to early casualties, including two elderly people injured in the darkness.

In August, the Lord Mayor of York, Alderman William Cooper, lent the Mansion House as a recruitment centre for national service. One man of 84 offered his services. Lads of 12 and 13 volunteered to be messengers and a blind man said he could act as a telephonist.

Meanwhile, a four-day operation to evacuate three million women, children and disabled people from the big cities got underway. Children from Hull and Leeds were sent to Pickering, Easingwold, Strensall, Boroughbridge and Haxby.

When hostilities did break out, the Evening Press produced a special edition. This carried news of the sinking by a German U-boat of the British Atlantic liner Athenia. It was bound for Canada with 1,400 passengers and crew.

Air raid shelters, ARP wardens' posts and first-aid centres were springing up across the city. The Yorkshire Evening Press revealed that 1,500 Anderson shelters, named after the Home Secretary Sir John Anderson, were on their way for families whose income did not exceed £250 a year, and who had gardens to put them in.

It printed advice on "how to build your own dugout", and which room to go to in the event of an air raid (the pantry). On the Monday morning after war was declared, most York people went to work carrying their gas masks.

By Wednesday, the Press was reporting "York Black-Outs Still Ineffective". Lieutenant Colonel Daly, the York ARP controller, said that in almost every street, light was coming from three or four skylights or back windows.

He said: "Speaking as Controller for the city, I cannot impress too strongly on all residents the vital necessity for ensuring that no light at all should be visible."

As the last months of the Thirties ebbed away, Britain adjusted to being at war. By the end of October, more than 50 German mines had been washed up on the Yorkshire coast.

In November, the Government announced that bacon and butter rationing was to be introduced. The Archbishop of York, Dr William Temple, said places of recreation and social intercourse were needed for evacuees.

A map of 23 air raid shelters, for shoppers and others too far away from other shelters, was published.

On November 11 – the first Armistice Day since war had broken out again – people stood in silence in York's streets. For the first time, all Army ranks were given permission to wear poppies while on duty.

Millennium Press

War!

Germany ignores Allies' ultimatum

BRITAIN was plunged into war with Germany today for the second time in two decades.

The German leader, Herr Hitler, has ignored an ultimatum from Britain and France to withdraw Nazi forces from Poland, and as a result Prime Minister Neville Chamberlain, in a broadcast to the nation at 11am today, said that a state of war now exists between Britain and Germany.

Britain is not unprepared for war, although Mr Chamberlain had hoped until the last minute that he and Herr

Local soldiers in York wait for their postings

Hitler could work out a deal similar to the one worked out in 1938, when Mr Chamberlain promised 'peace in our time.' It has proved to be a hollow promise.

Meanwhile, York is girding itself for action, as it seems certain that Germany's use of air power will bring the war to our doorsteps.

Air raid shelters, ARP wardens' posts and first aid centres are springing up across the city and 1,5000 Anderson shelters are on their way to the city.

Volunteers have been springing forward, including one man of 84 and a blind citizen who has offered to help as a telephonist. Boys as young as 12 or 13 have offered their services as messengers.

The German Air Raid on York
April 18, 1942

*I*T seemed a night like any other in wartime York. At midnight, all was quiet. Only the full moon – a bomber's moon – gave any clue to what the night was to hold. The German bombers - Junkers 88s and Heinkel 111s - approached York from the east. At 2.36am the codeword 'purple' alerted York's civil defence headquarters behind the Guildhall of the imminent attack.

There was no time for the city to take defensive action, even if defences were available. For already incendiary flares were dropping on York as markers for the bombs.

Then the city shook as the attack proper began. The first of nine massive one ton bombs exploded. With a chill of fear, residents realised that this was no drill.

York railway station was the major target. A 250 pound bomb crashed down at the far end. The 10.15pm Kings Cross to Edinburgh express was waiting at the platform; the soldiers and civilians sitting on board scrambled for cover.

Six coaches of the train were destroyed, as were the station's lamp room, parcels office, booking office and station master's office.

The German attackers went on to vent their full fury on the main line that ran in and out of York station. Buildings to the left and right suffered.

The Bar Convent was hit and two nuns were killed trying to rescue another. Manor High Grade School was totally destroyed; Poppleton Road, Shipton Street, Queen Anne's, Nunthorpe, Bootham and St Peter's Schools were all damaged.

York carriageworks was showered with high explosives. One struck the 'roundhouse' where 20 locomotives were parked around the central turntable. Some of the huge engines were tossed into the air by the blast, others were ripped open by shrapnel.

The beautiful church of St Martin-le-Grand in Coney Street was wrecked in the raid. Next door, the Evening Press building had been hit, as had the historic Guildhall.

Firemen from as far afield as Malton desperately tried to fight the blazes in New Street, Davygate, and the Leopard Arcade. Stretcher bearers from Rowntree's doubled back and forth carrying the casualties.

One York landmark to escape unscathed was the Minster.

Casualties were rising fast. With the emergency services fully occupied fighting fires and tending the seriously injured, the walking wounded had to fend for themselves.

Finally, the all clear sirens signalled the end of York's longest night. The German bombers departed, having done a comprehensive job of wrecking the ancient city. From Clifton airfield in the north-west to Fulford Barracks in the south-east, hardly a street escaped damage.

The human toll was inevitably high. Within the city boundary, 79 people were killed and 238 injured. A further 14 people died and seven were injured in the attack on Clifton airfield.

As dawn broke, and citizens emerged from their cellars and shelters, they discovered a city transformed. Glass and rubble was everywhere. Smoke filled the air.

The clear-up operation began immediately. A super-human effort saw the station up and running again within hours, with all lines available for use by the following evening.

York was physically devastated by the air raid in April 1942. But the enemy had singularly failed to break the people's spirit.

Millennium Press

April 18, 1942   **A thousand years of York's history**

War comes to York

German bombers devastate the city

Y ORK suffered its first serious raid of the Second World War today as German bombers rained death and destruction on the ancient city.

The main target was the city's railway station and vital railway links, with Clifton Aerodrome a secondary target.

Both were severely damaged, with the King's Cross-Edinburgh express hit while in the station, half a dozen carriages being destroyed. It was packed with servicemen at the time, but thankfully most scrambled clear.

York Station is a mass of tangled wreckage following the raid by German aircraft

Elsewhere in the city, the residents were not so lucky. Some 79 citizens - including two nuns - were killed and 238 injured. Another 14 died and seven were injured at Clifton.

Damage to the city was enormous. As well as the station, which was severely mangled, the city's ancient Guildhall, St Martin's Church in Coney Street, the Bar Convent and even the Evening Press offices were hit, as well as scores of houses across the city.

Despite the death and destruction, however, spirits are high and it is hoped to have the station operating again by tomorrow.

VE Day: the end of the Second World War nears
May 8, 1945

W E may allow ourselves a brief period of rejoicing," Mr Churchill said when hostilities ceased in Europe. The people of Britain did not need a second invitation.

For six long years, they had waited for the moment when the lights came on again. Victory in Europe Day was that moment.

As they had in 1918, the Minster bells pealed in celebration. The York Gas Company floodlit the great cathedral, a wonderful sight after years of blackouts.

Plans were hastily made to mark VE Day, which was declared a national holiday. The city was soon decorated with VE Day flags. Ten small flags on a streamer cost 15s 9d, or one large one set revellers back 19s 3d. The De Grey Rooms in Exhibition Square became a riot of red, white and blue.

Fears that York's pubs would be drunk dry were allayed by the brewers advancing their weekly deliveries. Children set about collecting firewood for celebration bonfires. Nazi effigies were prepared to be sacrificed on top.

Street parties and teas were laid on across the city. In Acomb, according to a rather ungallant report in the Evening Press, a group of 15-stone mums staged a sack race.

Children were enjoying special treats. At a party in Front Street, they were given one shilling, some sweets and an orange.

Many youngsters wore fancy dress. At the Clement Street party, girls dressed up as Bo Peep and, more topically, GI brides. After years of rationing, the spread of sandwiches, jelly and custard, buns and cakes looked fit for a king.

Irwin Avenue residents staged a fete with sports and fireworks. In a risqué development, women took part in an "ankle competition".

The spirit of the day even extended to York Magistrates Court. "This is rather a special day and we don't want to send you to prison on a day like this," chairman of the bench Mr GY Johnson told a defendant who had admitted theft and being drunk and disorderly. He was bound over for a year and ordered to leave the city but kept his freedom.

Later, crowds followed a pipe band down Micklegate. They surged into Parliament Street to listen to the VE Day broadcast, before descending en masse on the De Grey Rooms, where they sang and listened to music coming from inside the building.

Dancing took place all over York. The best value was Clifton Cinema ballroom at two shillings and sixpence, while tickets to the Albany Hall, the De Grey Rooms and the Grand Victory Dance were all five shillings apiece.

Life had changed in so many ways. On the eve of VE Day, the Yorkshire Evening Press was allowed to print an official weather forecast – the first since the start of the war. Public air raid shelters were closed. Residents were told to dispose of their own Anderson shelters.

But they had other things on their mind. For the first time in years, families could go on holiday. Motorists were servicing their cars ready for a summer break, although they had to be careful: it was possible to spend a month's petrol ration on a trip to Scarborough.

For some, however, the war was not over. Soldiers, sailors and airmen serving in the Far East still had three more months of hard fighting ahead before Japan surrendered and the Second World War was truly over.

Millennium Press

Victory in Europe!

Now only Japanese remain to be defeated

CITIZENS of York today launched a huge round of celebrations after it was announced that Germany had surrendered.

Prime Minister, Mr Winston Churchill, in announcing Germany's surrender, said, "We may allow ourselves a brief period of rejoicing."

He was referring to the fact that many thousands of British and Allied servicemen are stationed in the Far East where the war against Japan goes

Residents of Forest Grove, Heworth, hold a street party to celebrate Victory in Europe Day

on. Victory is near but Japan, as yet, shows no sign of surrendering.

Meanwhile in York, celebrations are well under way, with a peal of bells sounding in York Minster and plans to floodlight the cathedral now that the

blackout is ended.

Flags and bunting are everywhere and many will be able to raise a glass or two of beer to victory after brewers advanced their regular supply run to make sure the city pubs had plenty of ale.

The Great Freeze and Floods
1947

*T*HE bitter winter of 1947 began in the first week of January, when four inches of snow fell over York. It marked the start of a freeze that would last for two months. At its height, residents could not only walk across the Ouse in York, they could drive a horse and cart across it.

The snows left villages cut off, caused widespread shortages of fuel and food and cost many thousands of people their lives.

In an era before central heating, the lack of solid fuel caused a domestic and industrial crisis. The coal industry was transferred to the nation on January 1 by Prime Minister Attlee, and, from the start, the nationalisation process was hampered by shortages.

Electricity supplies to.York were cut off as measures to reduce voltage levels were introduced to save coal used in power stations.

War rations were still in place, with households limited to a sack of coal a week. Families were reduced to desperate measures to keep warm.

Coal dust was mixed with cement and burnt. Twigs were gathered and thrown on the fire. People even placed vegetable peelings on their coal to make it last longer. As the hardships continued, people were reduced to burning books and other possessions.

The weather was so bad that bread – which had gone unrationed during the war – was carefully apportioned by emergency food trains which were sent to the most isolated villages, and, by February, food containers were being dropped in by parachute from a bomber to more outlying areas.

Temperatures plunged as low as minus 22 degrees Fahrenheit. Washing hung out to dry would freeze on the line. With pumps frozen up, families were reduced to melting snow in the oven to provide water for drinking and washing.

Finally, in March, the thaw began. Surely now the population could relax. But more suffering was to come, in the resulting floods.

Rivers across the country burst their banks, but York – vulnerable to flooding at the best of times – was among the areas hardest hit.

The floodwaters rose quickly and with devastating effect. Residents of streets in the centre of the city moved upstairs en masse. Any furniture they could move was hauled up with them.

At its peak, the River Ouse was 16ft 4ins above its normal level. To escape, or simply to get around, people took to canoes and rowing boats. The council, Army and emergency services were working flat out to evacuate people, or deliver food to people staying in situ.

Selby was also devastated by the floods. Most of the town was underwater. The only dry area of any note was in the shadow of the Abbey.

Troops from Brayton Camp worked 16 hours a day running a ferry service, wading in waist deep water to rescue householders, and cooking for the hungry in the Market Square.

On the positive side, the response to the floods appeal was wonderful. Aid came in from as far away as Australia. And flood victims got a special surprise – a box with tins of fruit and dried fruit and vegetables from Princess Elizabeth.

Millennium Press

Under siege

**After the freeze come the floods: a dramatic picture of
Rougier Street under water**

THE misery of the terrible winter of 1947 will not be forgotten in the city of York and surrounding villages for a long time to come.

After weeks of snow, freezing temperatures and fuel shortages, the thaw has come and brought with it the misery of flooding.

It was only a few weeks ago that outlying villages

After the snows, floods descend on the city

were cut off by snow and food had to be dropped in by plane.

Now it is the turn of the towns and villages near the River Ouse to suffer as the Ouse burst its banks. At one time the river was 16ft 4ins above the normal

level and much of the centres of York and Selby are under water.

The council, Army and emergency services are working flat out to evacuate threatened householders and provide them with hot meals.

The first York Festival
1951

O NE hundred years after the Great Exhibition, Britain put on another show. The 1951 Festival of Britain celebrated the centenary and demonstrated the nation's returning confidence after the trauma of war.

As well as major events in London, Glasgow, Belfast and Cardiff, 22 provincial centres were to host festivities.

York won the right to be one of those centres. At the festival's heart was the revival of the York Mystery Plays. These 47 plays, telling the Bible story of mankind from the Garden of Eden to the Harrowing of Hell, had not been performed since 1580.

York's amateur theatrical societies were asked to help provide most of the 300-strong cast. The name of the actor chosen to play Christ was originally kept secret – in fact he was Joseph O'Connor, a 33-year-old, Dublin-born man.

It was announced that Mary Ure, a 17-year-old pupil of The Mount School, was to play the Virgin Mary. She later became a movie star: Where Eagles Dare, co-starring Clint Eastwood and Richard Burton, was one of her credits.

Dame Judi Dench, who was born in York and attended Britain's only all-girl Quaker school, The Mount, appeared in the Mystery Plays three times as a young actress, first as an angel, in 1951, then as the Angel of the Tomb in 1954 and, most famously, as the Virgin Mary in 1957. It was the latter role that set her on the road to stardom and awards galore.

Another ambitious part of the 1951 programme was the York Festival Flats. The Yorkshire Evening Press had explained the idea in June 1949: "A block of modern flats, outstanding in design, yet suitable for the ordinary man-in-the-street will be the modern architectural highlight of the 1951 Festival of York."

Two sites were chosen for new buildings, Paragon Street and Castlegate. The design of the Paragon Street flats was decided by an architectural competition.

Despite fears over spiralling costs and lack of time, the flats were all but completed in time for the Duchess of Gloucester to open them on June 4, 1951.

The Festival boasted classical music concerts at the Rialto, Fishergate, conducted by such luminaries as Sir John Barbirolli and Sir Adrian Boult.

Other events included: a Georgian costume ball at the Assembly Rooms; a production of 1066 And All That at the Theatre Royal; a flower show; a brass band contest; a river carnival; and an International Bicycle-Polo match between Scotland and Wales. An exhibition of locomotives and rolling stock drew crowds to York's old station.

Despite all the controversies, the delays, and the wrangles over plans and funds, the York Festival of 1951 was a genuine success.

The city itself had gained materially – the new flats and renovated Assembly Rooms are two examples. And the 1951 event was such a triumph that the idea was repeated in 1954 and 1957. There can be little doubt that this established York's status as a place to visit, starting a tourism boom which is still continuing.

Millennium Press

1951 **A thousand years of York's history**

City's Festival extravaganza

Mystery Plays revived as part of celebrations

LOCALS and visitors alike packed the city today to celebrate the 1951 York Festival and the revival of the city's famous Mystery Plays.

Many of the events, including the 47 plays in the Mystery Plays cycle, are being staged in the historic Museum Gardens, with the ruins of St Mary's Abbey providing a fitting backdrop.

Many local citizens are taking part with 17-year-old Mount School pupil Mary Ure taking the role of the Virgin Mary.

The Festival Flats are set to open in conjunction with the Festival, which also features musical and theatrical events at other venues around the city.

Crowds pack the Museum Gardens to watch one of the Festival's many cultural events

Queen Elizabeth II is crowned
June 2, 1953

*T*HE King was dead. Long live the Queen. George VI died in his sleep in Sandringham on February 6, 1952. His daughter was informed of her loss, and the fact that she was now Queen, on a tour of the Commonwealth with the Duke of Edinburgh. She was just 25.

The King's funeral took place at Windsor, his coffin carried there on a gun carriage.

Fifteen months later, on June 2, 1953, Queen Elizabeth II was crowned at Westminster Abbey by the Archbishop of Canterbury. It was a day of rejoicing for the whole nation. Fittingly, news broke early that morning that Edmund Hillary and Sherpa Tenzing Norgay had conquered Mount Everest, planting a Union Flag at its summit.

The day before, York had seen a last minute rush to find Coronation decorations. "Anything in red, white and blue or with 'God Save The Queen' on it was sold immediately. It was really astonishing," Mr Lyall, a Coney Street trader, told the Yorkshire Evening Press.

Heavy rain and winds on Coronation eve wreaked havoc with some of the street decorations. But undaunted by low clouds the following morning, street party organisers were up early repairing the damage.

With the threat of rain, some of the parties were hastily rearranged indoors. Many watched the grandeur of the crowning live on television. The sense of excitement and occasion was tangible wherever you went in the city.

Special services were held at every hospital in the city, with Rowntree's chocolates handed out to the children. A free variety show kept crowds amused on York Rugby League Club's ground at Wigginton Road. Races and other community entertainment was taking place in York's suburbs and in villages across North Yorkshire.

All babies born on the big day were given a presentation spoon by the City Council. The Civic Party read a loyal message to the Queen on the steps of the Mansion House.

In the evening, the Assembly Rooms hosted the glittering Civic Coronation Ball. The Lord Mayor Charles Oliver and Sheriff John Shannon were at the top table.

A ticket cost 30 shillings, but for that you got supper and a chance to dance until 3am. Dances included the Fox Trot and the Gay Gordons, with, inevitably, the Last Waltz to finish.

Nearby at the De Grey Rooms Johnny Sutton and his Modernaires were providing the music for the Coronation Carnival Ball. A River Gala brought to an end a glorious week in York.

The Queen's first visit to the city following her Coronation was in July, 1957. Before arriving in the city, she and Prince Philip attended engagements at the Great Yorkshire Show and Catterick Camp.

In York that evening, they were presented with a casket of chocolates by the Lord Mayor, Alderman E.L. Keld, at a reception in the Assembly Rooms.

After a private dinner of fish, roast lamb and soufflé at the Mansion House, the Queen and Prince Philip were due to watch a performance of the Mystery Plays. Unfortunately it was rained off, but they were later introduced to the cast at Tempest Anderson Hall.

Millennium Press

A new queen is crowned

Coronation of Queen Elizabeth II is celebrated

YORK joined the rest of Britain today in celebrating the coronation of Her Majesty, Queen Elizabeth II.

While the ceremony was being performed in Westminster Abbey by the Archbishop of Canterbury, York was celebrating the new monarch in its own way.

Although heavy rain and strong winds overnight caused havoc with street party arrangements, most citizens decided to go ahead with them anyway.

Some were transferred indoors but others braved the weather and community celebrations went on across the city.

And tonight citizens are prepared to dance the night away at a Civic Coronation Ball in the Assembly Rooms or with the Modernaires at a Coronation Carnival Ball at the De Grey Rooms.

The solemn moment in Westminster Abbey as Her Majesty Queen Elizabeth II is crowned

York City reach the FA Cup Semi-final

March 26, 1955

EVERY football fan loves a giant killer. And in the 1954/55 season, York City slew some whoppers. As Wilf Meek, sports editor of the Yorkshire Evening Press, stated in the souvenir of the team's astonishing cup run: "If anybody associated with York City had said three months ago that the club would be serious contenders for a place at Wembley, he or she would have been ridiculed."

In fact, the Third Division side came remarkably close to an appearance in the FA Cup Final.

Typically, the team nearly fell at the first hurdle. In the local derby, York scraped a 3-2 home win over non-league Scarborough. City were twice behind, and were fired into the second round when Ron Spence scored with four minutes to go.

An emphatic away win at Dorchester Town followed. The non-league club scored twice to City's five.

That won them a tie at mighty Blackpool, the 1953 FA Cup winners led by Stanley Matthews. Five thousand City fans saw their side triumph 2-0.

The fourth round saw York travelling again, this time to amateur club Bishop Auckland. Arthur Bottom scored twice in City's 3-1 victory.

"Now to the football classic of all time," Mr Meek wrote in his introduction to York City's match against Tottenham Hotspur.

In front of an all-ticket Bootham Crescent crowd of 21,000, and on a pitch made difficult by snow and ice, City put on a brilliant display. Despite going a goal down, they won 3-1.

More than 11,000 City supporters swelled the 47,301 crowd at Notts County in round six. Twelve minutes from time Bottom scored, sending the fans delirious with delight.

This saw the club into the FA Cup semi-final for the first, and so far only, time in their history.

On March 26, 1955, York City met Newcastle United on the neutral turf of Hillsborough. They came close: Bottom equalised after United had gone ahead, and City later missed an excellent chance to clinch victory.

The story came to an end in the replay at Roker Park four days later. City were handicapped throughout the second half by Alan Stewart's head injury (no substitutes were allowed) and they went down 2-0. So came to an end a remarkable season.

It wasn't the first time the minnows of York had enjoyed national sporting glory. In the 1930s, the decade which saw them move into Bootham Crescent from Fulfordgate, the team reached the quarter finals of the FA Cup.

Including replays, City played nine cup ties in the 1937/38 season, beating Halifax Town, Clapton Orient, Coventry City, West Bromwich Albion and Middlesbrough. The run came to an end when they were defeated 2-1 in a replayed tie at Huddersfield Town.

Middlesbrough were destined to finish fifth in the First Division and their visit to York ignited cup fever across North Yorkshire. The stand tickets at Bootham Crescent sold out in 90 minutes.

City won 1-0, with a terrific goal from Spooner which hit the bar before going in.

"Whoever gets to Wembley, there can be no greater display of enthusiasm there than witnessed at York yesterday," the Sunday Express match report stated.

Millennium Press

March 26, 1955   **A thousand years of York's history**

City's Wembley dream on hold

The York City team which today drew 1-1 with mighty Newcastle United at Hillsborough. The team is (back row, from left): Norman Wilkinson, Gordon Brown, Tommy Forgan, Alan Stewart, Ron Spence, George Howe and Tom Lockie (trainer). Front row: Billy Hughes, Arthur Bottom, Ernie Phillips, Sid Storey and Billy Fenton.

York forced to replay after 1-1 draw with Newcastle

YORK City's dreams of a first appearance at Wembley were put on hold today after the tiny Third Division North side drew 1-1 with Newcastle in their FA Cup semi-final tie at Hillsborough.

Despite the difference in league standing, City gave as good as they got and might well have won it, but they spurned a late chance to score the winner.

Now the two sides must meet again in a replay at Roker Park next week, although many pundits feel that City have had their best chance to make history and the might of Newcastle will tell in the end.

York's Royal Wedding: The Marriage of the Duke and Duchess of Kent
June 8, 1961

T HE next major royal occasion after the Coronation took place not in London, but in York. Katharine Worsley, the bubbly, country girl, became a Duchess in a dazzling wedding at the Minster. Soon afterwards the Duchess of Kent established herself as one of the best-loved members of the royal family. This came as no surprise to the people of Hovingham, who had watched young Katharine grow up.

The daughter of former Lord Lieutenant of the North Riding, Sir William Worsley, she had a vivacity and unaffected manner that won her many friends in the village. She never adopted airs and graces despite living at the impressive Hovingham Hall and being educated privately in Yorkshire, Norfolk and Oxford.

Villagers watched her romance with the Duke develop with discreet interest. It began perhaps four years before the 1961 wedding when the Duke, along with fellow officers from Catterick Camp, began visiting Hovingham Hall.

When their engagement was announced in March 1961 locals were delighted but not surprised. She showed off her diamond engagement ring to photographers and York Minster geared up for its first royal wedding since 1328.

Preparations for the big day were akin to those for a military operation. Police announced their decision to close most city streets to traffic from early in the morning.

York City Council's wedding sub-committee decided that bunting was vulgar and inappropriate. The streets would instead be decorated with flowers – 40,000 from the council alone.

Traders soon realised they could benefit from the interest in the marriage. A quarter of a million people were expected to line the streets. One store ordered 30,000 flags at sixpence each.

One London catering firm sent ten caravans to York to set up as mobile cafés. Rooms with windows overlooking York Minster were hired out for as much as £150.

Many less wealthy people spent all night on city pavements to secure a good position to see the wedding party arrive. The thousands in York were joined by millions of viewers watching the processions live on television.

Prince Michael of Kent, then 18, was best man and a young Princess Anne was among the bridesmaids. The Queen, the Duke of Edinburgh, Queen Mother and Prince Charles arrived at York station at 1.45pm, 45 minutes before the official start of the ceremony. They were taken on to the Minster by car.

Dressed in a dazzling gown with a train dozens of yards long, the bride was four minutes late at the West Door of the Minster. The sun shone as she alighted from the car to tremendous cheers. By the time she was inside the cathedral, a hail shower began.

The Duke was dressed in smart regimental scarlet and blue. They were married by the Archbishop of York, Dr Michael Ramsey.

The only surprise during the wedding itself was that the new Duchess used the word "obey" during the vows: a previous announcement insisted it would be omitted.

After the ceremony, the new husband and wife were met with cheers, flags and bunting all the way from York to the lavish reception in Hovingham.

Millennium Press

June 8, 1961   **A thousand years of York's history**

A Royal wedding

The Duke and Duchess of Kent leave York Minster after their wedding today

Local girl marries Duke of Kent in York Minster

MISS Katharine Worsley, daughter of Sir William Worsley of Hovingham Hall, near York, was married today to the Duke of Kent in York Minster.

The ceremony, performed by the Archbishop of York, Dr Michael Ramsey, was conducted in front of a host of Royal guests, including the Queen and Prince Philip, the Queen Mother and Prince Charles. Princess Anne was one of the bridesmaids and Prince Michael of Kent the best man.

After the service the couple left for Hovingham Hall for the reception - but not before a quick tour of the packed York streets to greet thousands of well-wishers.

The city itself was awash with flowers. The council's wedding sub-committee had decreed that bunting was 'common' so 40,000 blooms were used to decorate the city, while to ease traffic problems most of the city centre was closed for the day to motor vehicles not involved in the wedding.

York's 1900th birthday celebrations

1971

F EW cities boast a history as long and colourful as that of York – a point emphasised in 1971 when the people celebrated its 1,900th anniversary. In AD71 the Romans named their new outpost of empire Eboracum. For the next 19 centuries York was to witness violence and destruction, see its fortunes wax and wane and eventually develop culturally and commercially into the modern centre we know today.

A whole year's worth of events were organised to commemorate the birthday, from the New Year's Eve Ball in the Assembly Rooms to the December production of Handel's Messiah in York Minster.

The highlight was undoubtedly the visit of the Queen and Duke of Edinburgh to the city on June 28, 1971. They arrived, in heavy rain, through Micklegate Bar – the traditional royal entry point.

From their open carriage the Queen and Prince Philip acknowledged the cheers of the crowds, lined three or four deep. Their 60-strong escort came from the Household Cavalry, the first time it had ridden through York for 300 years.

The royal party had travelled to Rufforth in the morning by aeroplane before being driven to Knavesmire. As the Queen arrived, a 21-gun salute was fired, the blast rattling windows and causing some children to scream with fright.

A royal flypast of 21 Jet Provost aircraft was watched by the crowds. Then the Queen toured the silver enclosure, where there was a display of activities by children.

After travelling under Micklegate Bar on their way to lunch at the Assembly Rooms, the Queen and Prince Philip saw a 45-minute excerpt from the York Pageant which traced the city's history since it was founded by the Romans. Later, they hosted a garden party with 2,000 guests at the Museum Gardens.

Police had stepped up the already stringent security surrounding the royal visit after two threats were made to the Queen's life. Both were delivered to the Evening Press office purporting to be from the Angry Brigade.

Armed soldiers were on duty at Knavesmire, and police both in and out of uniform were issued with firearms. In the event, the day passed without incident.

Three months later another major event took place to mark York's 1,900th birthday. Probably the most spectacular event of the year-long celebrations, the six-day Services Searchlight Tattoo took place on Knavesmire in September.

A new fanfare, called Eboracum, was composed for the occasion by Captain Keith Boulding, director of music for the Royal Signals at Catterick.

It heralded a magnificent programme featuring no fewer than 520 musicians from nine service bands.

As well as RAF flypasts, crowds were treated to a Royal Military Police tent-pegging display; a performance by the Royal Army Veterinary Corps dog team; the Royal Signals motorcycle display team; and a jungle display by the Brigade of Ghurkas.

Around £1 million-worth of military hardware formed a static display on the Knavesmire all week. Exhibits ranged from a Thunderbird guided missile and a 50-ton Chieftain tank to a Navy Whirlwind helicopter. Even freshly baked buns from a field bakery were on show.

Millennium Press

Happy 1900th birthday!

City set to celebrate 19 centuries of history

York down the centuries is the theme of this float featuring members of York Townswomen's Guild

YORK has launched into a year-long celebration of the city's founding in AD71 by the Roman Army.

The city, originally named Eboracum, and later Eoforwic and Jorvik, has seen much of England's history during its long life and that will be celebrated in a variety of events during the year.

Festivities kick off with a special New Year's Ball in the Assembly Rooms and round off with a production of Handel's Messiah in York Minster in December.

In between, the highlight is a Royal visit by the Queen and Prince Philip.

The pair hope to go 'walk-about' in the city streets before being treated to a 45-minute excerpt from the York pageant, which traces the city's history since its foundation by the Romans.

Later the same day, they aim to host a Royal garden party, featuring 2,000 guests, in the Museum Gardens.

The other big event of the year is the six-day Services Searchlight Tattoo on Knavesmire, featuring £1million pound's worth of military hardware.

The Pope Visits York
May 31, 1982

A T 58, Pope John Paul II was the youngest Pope for over a century. Soon after his accession in 1978, he made the most of his comparative youth by travelling the world with a zeal never seen before.

Four years later John Paul announced he was coming to Britain. His visit was little short of miraculous – only 12 months earlier he had been gravely ill in hospital after being gunned down by a fanatic in Rome. Security for his British visit was therefore understandably tight.

At one stage it had looked as though the tour might be cancelled. The outbreak of the Falklands War threw it into doubt. His Holiness appealed to both Britain and Argentina to bring the conflict to a peaceful end. Then, after a few anxious days, he confirmed the visit was on.

The Pope arrived on British soil at Gatwick Airport on May 28, 1982. He bent to kiss the ground, by now a trademark of his papacy, before heading to take Mass at Westminster Cathedral.

Over the next three days, his schedule was relentless. He visited the Queen, held a service at Canterbury Cathedral, took Mass at Wembley, Coventry Airport and Liverpool Cathedral, and toured many destinations in between. Finally, York's big day, Bank Holiday Monday, May 31, 1982, arrived.

More than 2,000 pilgrims had spent the night at Knavesmire, the site of his visit. Thousands began to join them from the break of dawn onwards. Many had walked several miles after leaving their cars on Clifton airfield, even though dozens of park-and-ride services had been laid on. Some of the early birds took part in a special Mass that began at 7.30am.

Meanwhile, 26,000 people arrived on special trains. They made their way to Knavesmire in a vast human column.

On the way they could buy a whole range of official souvenirs from one of 30 stalls. Profits were earmarked to help offset the £1 million spent on the York visit. In the event, however, £220,000 of stock was left unsold.

A well-oiled police operation kept York itself a virtual traffic-free zone. The few city centre shopkeepers who had bothered to open waited forlornly for customers. The whole city, it seemed, was on the racecourse.

By the time His Holiness was due to arrive, some 210,000 people were gathered there. They were standing in 1,000-strong corrals, separated by crash barriers.

When his helicopter touched down on York turf, it was 2.08pm – he was 23 minutes late. He embraced the Archbishop of York, Dr Stuart Blanch, before climbing into the famed Popemobile to tour the huge crowd.

In his address to the York pilgrims, the Pope reaffirmed his belief in marriage and family life as the basis of society. And he prayed for the families in Britain and Argentina "who bear the heavy weight of pain and sorrow because of the loss of loved ones in the South Atlantic".

After he left York, heading for Edinburgh, the many thousands of pilgrims faced long delays to their journeys home. But they did so with a joyful heart, knowing that they had been there when history was made.

Millennium Press

May 31, 1982   **A thousand years of York's history**

History is made by the Pope

Crowds flock round His Holiness and the Popemobile on Knavesmire today

Huge crowds descend on Knavesmire for Papal visit

YORK'S historic Knavesmire has surely never seen a crowd like it: around a quarter of a million people heading for the green pastures for an historic visit.

It is believed that never before in the history of the Papacy has a Pope visited England during the term of his office.

But since John Paul II was elected Pope four years ago, he has made it papal policy to visit as many countries as possible.

Despite the fact that the Pope is still recovering from an attempted assassination attempt 12 months ago, he has followed a hectic schedule in the first three days of his British visit, meeting the Queen, holding a Mass at Wembley and services at Liverpool and Coventry and performing a host of other duties before coming to York.

Meanwhile Police have reported the city centre 'very quiet' while shopkeepers said trade was so slow it hardly seemed worthwhile opening.

York Minster Fire
July 9, 1984

W HEN the flames had finally been vanquished, and the firefighters collapsed in exhaustion, the enormity of the disaster began to sink in. York Minster was still standing, but only just. An incredible effort by more than 100 firefighters had prevented the blaze consuming the ancient structure.

But the damage was still severe. The roof of the 13th century South Transept lay in rubble on the ground. The fire that had broken out in the early hours caused £2 million-worth of damage.

It was not uncommon for a fire alarm to go off accidentally at the Minster. So the Red Watch at York Fire Station were unprepared for the sight they saw as they turned into Museum Street that night.

For a second they thought they had driven into fog. But then the realisation struck – it was smoke. As they got nearer they saw flames flickering from the roof. This was no false alarm.

Going into the great church, station officer Peter Wright saw hot embers falling from the roof. He immediately radioed for assistance. Crews from 13 stations across the region joined Red Watch to battle the fire.

For three long hours they worked to contain and eventually extinguish the conflagration. Their most frightening moment was when the roof fell in. Firefighters balanced on the escape staircase had to hang on tight to avoid being sucked down with the burning beams. But the collapse ensured that the flames did not spread to the rest of the church.

The Dean of York, Dr Ronald Jasper, who was due to retire a few days later, and some of the Minster canons went into the building to rescue some of the priceless treasures. They stripped the High Altar and the Lady Chapel Altar before thick smoke drove them out.

By dawn the fire was extinguished. Early sunlight illuminated a scene of devastation. The Minster was open to the skies. Church leaders entered the West Door to find themselves ankle deep in water. Charred beams smouldered at their feet. The walls and the stunning stained glass windows were blackened by smoke.

But at least the glass was safe. It would take years of painstaking restoration to return the Rose Window and the other glasswork back to their glorious best, but it was a project undertaken in good heart.

As the day wore on, two questions dominated the citizens' thoughts. How did the fire start? And what do we do now?

There is still not a satisfactory answer to the first question. After a lengthy investigation, lightning was singled out as the most likely reason; an electrical storm had been underway that night.

Some churchmen suggested it was a bolt from the Almighty, to signal His displeasure with the controversial views of the Bishop of Durham Dr David Jenkins. The Bishop had been consecrated in the Minster only days earlier.

The answer to the second question was simpler. Everyone rallied round to the cause. Cash came flooding in to the restoration appeal, and people from around the world offered their support.

Thus it was that, only four years later, the Queen came to York to officially re-open the restored South Transept. It was a Minster miracle.

Millennium Press

Blaze horror

The South Transept of York Minster blazes, threatening the precious stained glass in the Rose Window

YORK'S historic Minster came periously close to total destruction today after fire ravaged the South Transept.

Only the gallant efforts of more than 100 firefighters from 13 stations across the region saved the whole building from destruction.

As it is, the roof of the South Transept has been destroyed, and the famous Rose Window damaged by smoke and heat - although

Only desperate battle saves ancient cathedral

hopes are high the window can be restored.

Inside, a scene of devastation greets the visitor, with charred timbers all around and water sloshing about.

The fire is believed to have broken out in the early hours of this morning and no cause has yet

been established - although already there are claims that the fire was God's way of showing His displeasure over the ordination of the controversial Bishop of Durham, Dr David Jenkins, which took place in the Minster days earlier.

North Yorkshire mourns Princess Diana

August 31, 1997

*A*S we awoke on that last Sunday of summer in 1997, we could not imagine the news that was about to confront us. For many, the first indication was the sombre tones of the national anthem played out over the radio airways. The headline that followed was as brutal as it was unexpected: "Diana, Princess of Wales, died early this morning after the car she was travelling in crashed in Paris."

It was impossible, a sick joke. Princess Diana, the most famous woman in the world, had gone. One demented moment in a road tunnel had cost the life of this 36-year-old icon, her companion Dodi Fayed and the chauffeur Henri Paul.

Immediately the tributes poured in. The Dean of York, the Very Reverend Raymond Furnell, called her death a tragedy and prayed for her family at a service in York Minster. The Lord Lieutenant of North Yorkshire, Sir Marcus Worsley, said: "Like everyone else, I am shattered to hear this news. My first thoughts are for those two boys who are at such a vulnerable point in their lives."

Stunned staff at the Evening Press came into work early on Sunday morning to produce a special edition of the paper which hit the news stands later that morning. Even then, people reading the special edition seemed unable to take it in.

Diana's death was followed by the most extraordinary week in recent history. Britain was convulsed by an outbreak of mass mourning on a scale not seen before. The grief was genuine, tangible and largely unexpected.

Thousands of people queued up to sign books of condolence at the Mansion House in York and at Selby Abbey. A single candle was lit in the princess's memory at York Minster, which became a focal point for grief.

On the day of the funeral, the normally bustling city streets were eerily silent as York woke up to a fittingly gloomy day. A sense of anticipation hung in the air as people emerged to face one of the saddest days many had known.

Hundreds of people packed into York Minster to watch the moving funeral procession on four television screens. They saw Princes Charles, William and Harry walk behind the coffin through London to Westminster Abbey. There Sir Elton John paid his musical tribute, Goodbye England's Rose. North Yorkshire soprano Lynne Dawson, a former member of the York Chapter House Choir, gave a faultless rendition of Verdi's The Requiem.

Earl Spencer paid a heartfelt tribute to his sister in a funeral oration that openly criticised the royal family but drew applause from the congregation and mourners outside the abbey.

The day after the funeral, thousands of mourners paid their respects to Princess Diana at a special commemorative service in York Minster. In a moving tribute, the Archbishop of York, Dr David Hope, urged people to look at themselves and follow Diana's charitable example towards others.

"Perhaps there is a clear message about the nature of society and the nature of relationships where respect and courtesy and compassion might seem a better model than the often brutish self-interest and self-regard which can so often characterise our dealings with one another," he said.

More than 3,400 people of all ages filled the Minister, with another 800 in nearby St Michael-le-Belfrey Church, and hundreds of others in Dean's Park where loudspeakers relayed the service.

Millennium Press

Princess Diana dies in car crash

Paris tragedy claims life of 'Queen of Hearts'

AN HORRIFIC car crash in a Paris underpass today claimed the life of Diana, Princess of Wales. Her companion, Dodi Fayed, son of Harrods' millionaire owner Mohammed Al Fayed, and the car's driver, Henri Paul, were also killed. Another Al Fayed employee who was in the car - bodyguard Trevor Rees-Jones - is seriously ill in hospital.

It is believed that the couple were trying to outspeed chasing paparazzi after a night out on the town, when the driver lost control and the car struck the concrete wall of the underpass.

The shock of the princess's death immediately struck home in York. The Dean, the Very Reverend Raymond Furnell, called the death a tragedy and prayed for the family at a service in York Minster, while Sir Marcus Worsley, Lord Lieutenant of North Yorkshire, said: "My first thoughts are for those two boys who are at such a vulnerable point in their lives."

Books of condolence are to be placed in York Mansion House and Selby Abbey.

Princess Diana, who was killed earlier today in a car crash in Paris

The great River Derwent floods

March, 1999

SNOW was melting on the North York Moors as winter gave way to spring. Then a low pressure weather system lodged itself over the North Sea, causing the heavens to open. It was a disastrous climatic combination. The rain kept coming until the inevitablè happened: the River Derwent burst its banks. Large areas of Malton, Norton, Pickering, Stamford Bridge and Elvington were underwater. Pubs, shops, businesses and homes were devastated. Farmers' crops were ruined.

By Tuesday, March 9, the Derwent at Malton was 19 metres deep, 3.5 metres higher than the average for the time of year and breaking the previous record of 18.6 metres in 1931. Downstream at Stamford Bridge, the river peaked at ten metres deep, breaking another record.

Dozens of residents were evacuated, some by boat. Food and beds were provided by North Yorkshire County Council at Malton and Norton Colleges. Schools were closed.

But the floods failed to dampen community spirit. Friends, relatives, council staff and the voluntary services all rallied round to help the flood victims with food and shelter.

Volunteers even waded through the water to deliver the Evening Press with its latest news on the catastrophe.

Throughout it all, life went on – literally in the case of expectant mum Jane Hartley. Unable to get through the flood waters to reach York District Hospital to give birth, Jane and partner Geoff Hutchinson, from Appleton-le-Moors, made it to Malton Hospital instead. There the first water baby of the floods was born. She was later named Miranda, after Prospero's island-bound daughter in Shakespeare's play The Tempest.

On the Wednesday, March 10, agriculture minister Elliot Morley toured Malton and indicated that the Government would look favourably on any application for emergency funding for the flood-hit areas.

The following day brought even more welcome news. Floodwaters were starting to subside. However, this only revealed the scale of the damage. To put the area right would cost £100 million, experts estimated.

Police patrols were stepped up in Malton and Norton as fears grew that looters would be tempted to target flood-damaged properties while they stood empty.

A day later the rain stopped, and the great clean-up operation started. Tide marks on the walls of homes attested to how high the waters had risen. Furniture, carpets and decor were ruined. It would take months to put right.

A flood relief fund was started and quickly raised thousands of pounds. Donations came in from the other side of the world, after people read about the disaster on the Internet.

When the Duke of York toured the region early the following week, it was bathed in bright sunshine. But the effects of the disaster were all too obvious.

He met flood victims in Malton and Norton before travelling on to Stamford Bridge. In each town he talked to the worst affected, helping to lift their spirits.

Later, the Environment Agency announced a major revamp of its flood warnings after admitting there was widespread confusion during the disaster.

The floods served as a timely reminder to all. However far man has advanced in the last Millennium, and in the last century in particular, Mother Nature always has the last word.

Millennium Press

March, 1999   **A thousand years of York's history**

A drowned land

Floodwaters from the swollen River Derwent menace the village of Old Malton

Countryside under water as swollen River Derwent bursts its banks

A GREAT swathe of Ryedale and East Yorkshire is under water after the River Derwent, swollen by melting snows and torrential downpours, burst its banks.

As well as thousands of acres of prime farmland, the towns of Malton, Norton, Pickering and Stamford Bridge, as well as a host of smaller villages, have been severely hit by rising floodwaters.

In Malton the Derwent was 19 metres deep, 3.5 metres above normal and a new record height. Large parts of the town and Norton were flooded and residents were evacuated, some by boat, and food and beds were provided for them by North Yorkshire County Council.

Elsewhere, friends and neighbours rallied round with offers of food, clothing and accommodation. In some areas volunteers even waded through the floodwaters to deliver the Evening Press!

Despite the heightened community spirit, many residents have voiced complaints about the lack of early warning and the Enviroment Agency has promised to review its flood warnings system.

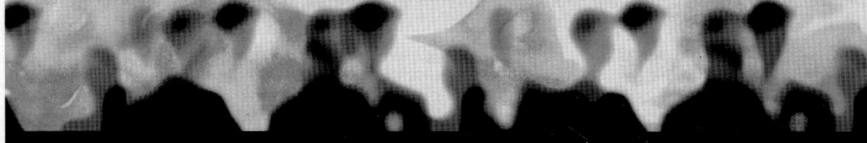